Granny Square

Flair

UK Terms Edition

50 Fresh, Modern Variations
of the Classic Crochet Square

Shelley Husband

ISBN-13: 978-0-6483497-0-9

Charts made by Amy Gunderson

Email: kinglouiespizza@gmail.com
Ravelry ID: AmyGunderson

Graphic Design by Michelle Lorimer

Email: hello@michellelorimer.com

Project Photography by Jo O'Keefe

Email: jookeefe@hotmail.com
Instagram: missfarmerjojo

Other Photography by Shelley Husband

Technical Editing by SiewBee Pond

Email: essbee1995@yahoo.com

First edition 2018

Published by Shelley Husband
PO Box 11
Narrawong VIC 3285
Australia
www.spincushions.com

Contents

The Dahlia Scarf, page 85.

The Heirloom Sampler Blanket, page 97.

Welcome to Granny Square Flair!

I love nothing more than sitting down with some yarn and my hook to design new granny squares. I love the problem solving, the Eureka! moment when an idea comes to life, trying out new yarns and colours. It's all so much fun. Granny Square Flair was born from this joyful exploration. I've gathered fifty of my original designs in this book, taking the humble granny square in exciting new directions.

The textbook definition of a granny square is a square piece of fabric textile crocheted while working in rounds from the centre outwards. I prefer to describe them as bite-sized adventures in yarn where you get to play with lots of different stitches and techniques to create little bits of joy. You can then combine them to make all manner of wonderful things.

Making crochet squares is gratifying in so many ways. They give you a sense of achievement, since you can complete a square easily in one sitting. You get to do a little happy dance every time you finish one. There's no boredom caused by working endless rows all the same. Plus, you'll reap the many benefits of keeping your mind and your hands happily occupied creating something beautiful.

If all that isn't enough, granny squares are the perfect portable project. They're great for the daily commute, or for when you're in the passenger seat on road trips. Treat them as a break in your busy day, your "relax and forget about the world" time. If you make a granny square every day or so, you'll have enough for a whole project in no time at all!

The patterns in this book run the gamut from quick and easy to those requiring a little more concentration. I've assumed that you have basic crochet skills. This is not a learn to crochet book, but rather a resource to create your own projects, expanding your skills and confidence as you play with the patterns.

In addition to the patterns for the fifty squares, you'll find complete instructions for eleven beautiful projects you can make with them. But don't limit yourself to these projects. My hope is that you use these patterns in ways that mean something to you, to make what you want. To that end, I've provided guidance on designing your own projects as well.

I hope my book will inspire you to try new techniques, expand your crochet skills and create some crochet wonders you and your loved ones will cherish for years to come.

Now go swing that hook!

xx Shelley

What you need to have

Let's have a look at the supplies you'll need to have on hand.

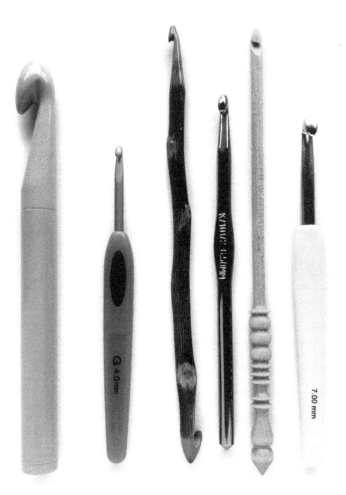

Hooks

While the business end of crochet hooks is fairly standard, their design and construction vary greatly. Some are a simple shaft and hook but others have handles of many shapes and sizes. They can be made of many different materials too, from metals to woods to plastics and combinations of all of these.

If you're going to spend a lot of time crocheting, investing in a good set of hooks can make the experience so much more pleasurable, allowing you to crochet for long periods of time comfortably. The hook you choose will depend on your personal preferences and crochet style. Some suit the overhand/knife hold, while others are best for the underhand/pen hold.

Regardless of hook style, the size I recommend for the patterns in this book is 4 mm/G if you're using 8 ply/DK/light worsted yarn.

Of course you're not bound by this! Experiment!

If you want to use a thicker 10 ply/aran/worsted yarn or a thinner yarn like a 2 or 4 ply/fingering, go for it. Begin with the hook size recommended on the yarn label. If you like the density and drape of the pattern, great! Continue on. If you want a firmer, stiffer fabric, use a smaller hook. Conversely, if you want a lacier fabric with more drape, use a larger hook.

Changing the yarn and hook from what I've recommended can result in squares of a different size. That doesn't matter unless you're making garments or matching my patterns with those from other sources. A blanket is a blanket no matter the size. If you use a heavier weight yarn and larger hook, your end product will be larger, and it will be smaller with a lighter yarn and smaller hook. The amount of yarn required will change a little as well as the size. Do your calculations at the beginning of your project and all will be well.

Yarn

Ah yarn. So much to choose from! There are many factors that will influence your yarn choice.

Fibre

Yarns are constructed from many different fibres; cotton, wool (sheep, alpaca, angora, cashmere, yak), linen, bamboo and man-made fibres like acrylic and nylon. Allergies may exclude some fibres from your selection. Man-made fibres and some yarn processing methods may conflict with your environmental values, excluding others.

Construction

How each yarn is constructed can also impact your choice. A yarn with a low twist may be prone to split making it difficult to crochet with. A more tightly twisted yarn may produce a stiffer, less flexible fabric. A fluffy yarn will hide intricate stitches, whereas a cotton yarn will show each stitch clearly.

Cost

Cost can be a big part of your yarn decision, especially when you consider the quantities of yarn needed for larger projects. It's a good idea to think about the time and love you'll be investing in your project. Investing in a lovely yarn as well will mean loving the end result so much more.

Project

The purpose of your project should influence your yarn choice. If you're making a pet blanket, then an easy-care acrylic may be your go-to yarn. A baby blanket needs to be soft and easy to wash, so a blend may work best. If you're making a bag, you may want to use a mercerised cotton yarn for added durability. What is best for you and your project will depend on your personal preferences. Personally, I love soft, non-mercerised 8 ply/DK/light worsted cotton yarns because I make mostly blankets and I love the soft drape and stitch definition this yarn yields. No one wants to snuggle under a scratchy, stiff blanket!

You'll need to decide what yarn best suits your personal preferences, budget and purpose.

Other useful things to have

- A nice sharp pair of scissors
- A tapestry needle
- A tape measure
- Stitch markers (scraps of yarn work just fine)
- Blocking board and pins

What you need to know

Now let's have a look at the technical "how-to's" with a bit of an explanation of how to begin, my seamless crochet tips and tricks, notes about size, playing with colour and how to read my patterns and charts.

How to begin a Square

There are many ways to begin a Granny Square. Most of the time, I recommend you begin with chain 1 and work all round 1 stitches into that 1 chain. After finishing, use the tail to pull the hole in the centre closed as you weave the end in.

However, due to the large number of stitches in the first round of some patterns, it's necessary to make a loop to work the first round stitches into. You can either make a length of chain stitches and join them with a slip stitch to make a loop or use a magic circle. If you do choose to use a magic circle, ensure you weave in the tail very securely as magic circles may come undone with use or washing.

Each pattern states which method to use.

Chain 1

Chain loop

Magic circle

My Seamless Crochet Tips

To help make your crochet look the best it possibly can, use my tips to create seamless joins and easy transitions between colours and rounds. Each of these tips by itself doesn't make much of a difference, but in combination, they go a long way to help create the illusion of seamless crochet.

Starting chain alternative

The traditional way to begin a round of crochet is to start with a number of chain stitches that generally take the place of the first stitch. For example, if a treble crochet stitch is needed at the start of a round, it's traditional to chain 3 to take the place of the first stitch. This matches the height of a treble stitch and you're at the right place to begin the next stitch i.e. from the top down.

This starting chain can really stand out as different from other stitches when worked in the round, so to make that first stitch blend in I make a false stitch instead.

Here's how to do it.

Pull up a long loop, a little taller than a treble crochet stitch (A). Place a finger on the loop on the hook and hold it firmly while moving the hook under, and wrapping the long loop around the hook (B). Yarn over and pull that strand under the wrapped long loop (C), yarn over again and pull through all remaining loops on the hook (D). It may look a little strange, but once you work the next stitches of the round, it will blend in nicely. At the end of the round, when it's time to join, you can join under 2 loops, just as if you were working into a regular stitch (E).

The false stitch is not limited to a treble crochet. You can also create a false double treble crochet by pulling up a longer loop and wrapping it twice around the hook before finishing the stitch as normal.

It does take some practice to perfect, but the result is well worth the effort.

However, there are times when a starting chain is still the best option. When it's necessary to finish a round with an invisible join, a starting chain is best as the top of the invisible join and the starting chain together create a stitch that looks very much like a normal stitch.

A

B

C

D

E

When a half treble is required at the beginning of a round, a starting chain of 2 is the easiest option. It's possible to create a false half treble, but it's very fiddly to do and not really necessary as the stitch is so short, you can't really notice the difference using a starting chain.

All patterns in this book indicate starting chains, but you have the option to use the false stitch alternative if you wish.

Changing colours

When starting a new colour, it's generally best to attach your new colour to a different stitch or space to where you ended the last round.

Joining methods

I recommend a mix of the following methods to join a new colour.

Slip Stitch

The first is to attach the new colour with a slip stitch, then either make the starting chain or a false stitch, as you prefer.

Standing Stitch

The second is to attach the new colour with a standing stitch. A standing stitch is created by attaching your new colour yarn to your hook with a slip knot then working the stitch as normal.

Attaching with a slip stitch is recommended when there is only one round of that colour, as using a standing stitch will result in having to weave in two ends at the same place at the end of the round. Joining with a slip stitch in this instance means you have one end to weave at the base of the round and one at the top of the round.

Where rounds end and begin

It's quite normal in crochet patterns to have to slip stitch to the corner, to have to work backwards a little to begin the next round, or to begin and end each round in the middle of a side which leaves a visible seam. These options are fine in some patterns, but it can be problematic in others.

Depending on the pattern, the slip stitches can be visible if the stitches you slip stitch into are not worked into in the next round. If they are worked into, it can be more difficult to get your hook into those stitches and it also creates a little more bulk in that section.

To combat the need to slip stitch to the correct place, having to work backwards a little to begin the next round or having a visible seam, my patterns use a technique borrowed from doily patterns.

A lot of doily patterns are made with long chain loops with a single stitch worked into the middle of those long chain loops in the next round. To avoid the need to slip stitch many times to reach the centre of a long chain loop, which would create a much thicker section that would stand out, these patterns are joined with a stitch. For example, if there was a round of 7-chain loops, the last 7-chain loop may be created by chaining 3 then joining with a double treble crochet. This places your hook as if it's in the middle of the 7-chain loop, in the right place to make a stitch for the next round. The double treble pretends to be the second half of the 7-chain loop.

I use this methodology when designing my squares. In the case of a square with 2-chain corner spaces, the round will end with the instruction to chain 1 and join with a double crochet. That double crochet takes the place of the second chain and places your hook at exactly the right spot to begin the next round, with no need to slip stitch or work backwards. Depending on the pattern, you may be instructed to work a stitch over that joining stitch. Treat the joining stitch as the second chain of the 2-chain corner space and work over it as if it were a chain loop.

If the corners of the pattern are larger chain loops, the final number of chains to be worked and the joining stitch will be different. For example, if a round has corners of 4-chain spaces, it may end with chain 1, join with a treble crochet. A round with 3-chain spaces may end with chain 1, join with a half treble crochet.

To make it easy to see where to place your hook in the next round after joining with a stitch, it may help to place a scrap of yarn in the corner gap before you join. This scrap of yarn shows you where to place your hook if you need to work over a joining stitch and where to work the last stitch/es of the next round.

Joining with a stitch means you're beginning each round, when square, on the diagonal, i.e. half of the first corner is worked, then the four sides and other three corners, then the first corner is finished at the end of the round. Joining at this point eliminates having a visible seam on a side.

Of course, as with most rules, there will be the occasional exception. There are a couple of patterns in this book where a slip stitch is used before beginning a round to avoid over-complicating the pattern.

Size

All patterns in this book measure 15 centimetres/6 inches when made with 8 ply/DK/light worsted yarn and a 4 mm/G hook, if your tension is average.

A small difference in size won't matter unless you're using patterns from this book to match with patterns from other sources. Your end result (blanket, bag, cushion, scarf) could turn out to be a little larger or smaller, but unless you're making garments, it doesn't matter. A small difference in each square, even with the largest blanket won't mean a huge overall different end result. If you're only using a single pattern for an entire project, it won't matter as all your squares will be the same size.

If you use just patterns from this book and the same yarn and hook throughout, your squares are all likely to be about the same size.

However, there may be instances where you may find a square is more than a little different in size to what you need. Let's look at why it may happen and what you can do to correct size issues.

Different yarn

Not all yarns are equal - even among "equivalent" yarns. For example, while the yarn I used for the cream samples and the blue samples are theoretically equivalent, the blue squares were generally a little smaller than the cream squares.

Crochet style

While all my squares resulted in blocked squares measuring 15 centimetres/6 inches, you may find small variations in size due to your crochet style. Take the Deco pattern as an example. This pattern uses mostly double treble crochet stitches. These are large stitches and if your tension for double trebles is different to mine, it could end up a lot larger or smaller. The same may be true for any pattern that uses a lot of one particular stitch.

Ways to match size

If you do need to ensure your squares are the same size, there are a few things you can do to make that happen.

Joining

The process of joining can even out small size differences if a solid join is used.

Blocking

Blocking works well when a square is a little smaller than other squares.

Adjust the pattern

If you need to add size, you can either add a round of double crochet or adjust the type of stitches in the last round to make it larger. For example, if a pattern ends with a round of half treble crochet, change it to a round of treble crochet to add some size.

If the square is a little too big, there are some patterns where you can leave off the last round without affecting the pattern. Otherwise, you can change the type of stitches in the last round to smaller stitches.

Hook Size

If a square turns out too large, tackling the pattern again using a smaller hook size can be a good option. Conversely, using a larger hook will make the square larger if that is what you need.

Colours

A note on hook and square size

While the recommended hook size for 8 ply/DK/light worsted yarn is a 4 mm/G hook, you're not bound by that. The same goes for any recommended yarn weight and hook combinations.

Try a smaller hook for a denser, stiffer fabric or a larger hook for a lacy fabric with more drape. Use the hook size that gives you the result you want. As long as you're consistent, all will be well. Of course the size of your squares will be larger or smaller depending on what you do, but as we've discussed, it doesn't matter.

All patterns in this book are written with no colour changes, and are shown in Parchment Bendigo Woollen Mills 8 ply Cotton. However, changing colours to suit your preferences is encouraged.

Should you wish to change colours and the round is joined with a stitch as explained in the seamless section, a small alteration to how you end the round will be needed. Simply chain the same number as the other corners/chain loops of the round and join with a slip stitch to the first stitch or starting chain.

As well as the single colour version, each pattern shows at least two of the many ways you can play with colour. Luckily for me, some of my crochet friends from around the world have helped me out by making a square using their favourite colours and yarns. Keep an eye out for these special contributions.

Of course, you can do anything you like when it comes to colour. Each square could be made using any number of colours from one to as many colours as there are rounds. Express yourself by using your favourite colours or colours that match your decor. Experiment and see what you like. Try alternating colours every couple of rounds, or crocheting a rainbow. There really are so many options and each will create a new look for the same pattern.

If you find it hard to choose colours, do a spot of research on colour theory at your local library or online. Just remember there is no right or wrong with colour. There is only what pleases you and what doesn't.

How to read the patterns and charts

Let's have a look at what you'll find on every pattern page.

Pattern Information

Symbols

Difficulty rating - 1 ball and hook is easy, 2 is intermediate, 3 is more advanced

Yarn requirements - the amount of yarn in metres needed to make one square using 8 ply/DK/light worsted yarn and a 4 mm/G hook.

Infinity symbol - this means that the pattern can be repeated endlessly, increasing the number of stitches each round to create a square as large as you desire. Notes to extend these squares are included.

Notes / Special Stitches / Tips

If there is anything unusual about a pattern or a special stitch or technique is used, it will be explained at the top of the pattern page.

Written pattern

Here's an excerpt from a pattern;

R1: ch3 (stch), 2tr, *ch2, 3tr*, rep from * to * 2x, ch1, join with dc to 3rd ch of stch. {12 sts, 4 2-ch sps}

R2: dc over joining dc, *dc in next 3 sts**, (dc, ch2, dc) in 2-ch sp*, rep from * to * 2x and * to ** 1x, dc in same sp as first st, ch1, join with dc to first st. {5 sts on each side; 4 2-ch cnr sps}

R3: ch3 (stch), tr over joining dc, *2x [tr in next st, ch1, skip 1 st], tr in next st**, (2tr, ch2, 2tr)*, rep from * to * 2x and * to ** 1x, 2tr in same sp as first sts, ch1, join with dc to 3rd ch of stch. {7 sts, 2 1-ch sps on each side; 4 2-ch cnr sps}

At the start of a round, I tell you how to begin, then you'll see an asterisk. This single asterisk indicates the beginning of a repeat. Ignore it and keep working following the instructions until you get to "rep". That is your cue to go back to the first single asterisk and repeat the stitches after it as instructed. After the repeats are done, I tell you how to finish off the round.

The instructions between a single asterisk and the double asterisks equal one side only. The instructions between the double asterisks and single asterisk equal one corner. So that means the instructions between the first and last single asterisks equal one side and the following corner. This is true of a square pattern but it also works for sections of patterns that begin as other shapes.

In those cases, the instructions between the single asterisks are a full pattern repeat and those from the single asterisk to the double asterisks are a partial repeat.

Brackets

(xxxxx) are stitches and/or chain spaces that are either to be all worked in the one stitch or space as indicated, or a set of stitches and/or chain spaces to be skipped.

[xxxx] indicate a small set of stitches and/or chain spaces to be repeated within a pattern repeat. These brackets will be preceded with a number and x to indicate how many times to work the small repeat. E.g. 2x [xxxxxx] means to work the [stitches and/or chain spaces] twice.

{xxxx} contain the stitch count for each round. This states how many stitches are along each side between the corners and describe the corners.

If the pattern begins as a shape with no corners, then it describes how many stitches in total make up that round.

It really does pay to check the stitch count every now and then, especially if you're about to square off a circle. It's important to have the right number of stitches or it just won't work.

NOTE: if there is a number of chain stitches at the start of a round not followed by (stch) they are not counted in the stitch counts. These are not a starting chain, but rather an aid to getting your hook to the right place to begin the round and will be invisible once the round is complete. Slip stitches to join rounds are also not counted in the stitch counts. However, if they are used in a pattern repeat, slip stitches are included in the stitch counts.

Charts

The charts are visual representations of the written patterns. Each stitch of the pattern is represented by a symbol. You'll find a key for all the symbols in the glossary in the references section.

Sometimes it may be best to work with the chart and written pattern in conjunction, especially when stitches are worked into earlier rounds or behind other stitches as it's difficult to show multiple layers in the charts. Conversely, there will be occasions when referring to the chart can make it easier to understand the written pattern.

Other things to note about the written patterns

If you need to skip stitches or chain spaces, it will be specifically stated in the pattern. E.g. skip next 2 sts, or skip (3 sts and 2-ch sp).

If you need to work into rounds other than the previous round, it will be referred to by R#. If no round is stated, then the instructions refer to the previous round only. A pattern may instruct you to work into more than one earlier round in the same round.

Finishing Tips

To help your crochet projects look fantastic, here are a few tips from me, as well as some options for joining and adding a border to your projects.

Blocking

To make your squares sing, blocking is recommended for all of your squares. It's especially good for lacy squares, as it makes the negative space created by the stitches really stand out. It can also help with slight size differences if a square turns out a little bit smaller than others. The joining process will help the straightening process, but blocking first is still recommended.

Here are the most common methods:

Steam blocking

Pin out to size on a foam mat or blocking board and hover your hot iron over your square, squirting it with steam. Leave to dry.

Wet Blocking

Following the care instructions for your yarn, gently hand wash your square, pin out to size on a foam mat or blocking board and leave to dry.

Joining

There are many joining methods in crochet. The internet is full of great examples. Some notable joins are Flat Braid Join, Mattress Join and Whip Stitch Join. The join you choose will depend on the result you're after. I've used the following three methods in this book.

Double Crochet on Back

This join is perfect for squares of the same colour, or if the same colour is used to end each square. It's lovely and flat on the front and it leaves a ridge on the back that is not noticeable.

Hold squares right sides together, attach joining yarn with a standing double crochet to both 2-chain corner spaces on each square at the same time. Work a double crochet into both loops of both squares all the way along, end with a double crochet in both 2-chain corner spaces. Fasten off.

Join the squares into strips, then join the strips as the squares were joined but when you reach the 2-chain corner spaces, work one stitch in each, ignoring the join. This creates a neat square on the front of the work in the 2-chain corner spaces.

To make the joining a little easier, it's possible to join the squares into strips as you make them if you're using the same colour to end each square and know your layout. Here's how:

Complete one square as normal.

With subsequent squares, end with chain 1, join with double crochet to first stitch or starting chain. Hold this square and completed square, right sides together, double crochet over joining double crochet and into 2-chain corner space of first square at same time, double crochet in all stitches of both squares, double crochet in 2-chain corner spaces of both squares. Fasten off. Repeat until you have a strip long enough for your project. Once you have your second and subsequent strips, you can join them as above.

Double Crochet on Front

For a visible and decorative join, you can use this join as the ridges are on the front. Perfect for joining squares made with different colours. You can use a high contrast colour for a dramatic, framing effect.

Hold squares wrong sides together, attaching joining yarn with a standing double crochet to both 2-chain corner spaces on each square at the same time. Work a double crochet into both loops of both squares all the way along, including the 2-chain corner spaces. Do not end the join after joining two squares, instead continue with the next two squares to be joined and so on until you have joined the entire width. Then join the squares in the other direction. Doing this means there are no breaks in the joining lines on the front.

Note as this join is visible, make sure you work in the same direction vertically and then horizontally as the join will lean slightly to one side. Making sure you do this will mean it looks uniform.

Zipper Join

This join works well for joining squares regardless of what colours are used.

Place two squares right sides up, next to each other. Beginning in the chain stitches, slip stitch through the back loops only of stitches of both squares through the front from the bottom of both squares to the top, ending in the chains. Fasten off.

A word about stitch counts

Most of the fifty patterns in this book have a final stitch count along the sides of 21 or 23 stitches. The rest range from 20 to 27 stitches. It's easy to deal with this difference if you join using the joins I've explained here.

If the stitch counts are different, simply use a stitch on the shorter square twice while using new stitches on the longer square as you join. This can be repeated as many times as needed. Spread the double stitches out a little so they are not all together. For example, if you were joining a 23-stitch square to a 21-stitch square, you'd use the same stitch on the shorter square twice. Make one double stitch on the shorter square a few stitches after starting to join and then the other double stitch near the end of joining. If you were joining a 23-stitch square to a 27-stitch square, you'd use the same stitch twice four times on the shorter square. Space the four double stitches out roughly evenly as you join.

Border

Once you have joined your squares, you'll need to add some kind of border to neatly finish your work. There are entire books devoted to different ways to edge crochet. You can go wild, adding fancy borders or you can keep it simple. If you're wanting to frame your work, a plain border does the job nicely. I used this border on my sampler blankets.

A Simple Border Pattern

R1

Attach main colour yarn with a stdg dc to any 2-ch cnr sp, *dc in each st on side, working a dc in each 2-ch sp and join**, (dc, ch2, dc) in 2-ch cnr sp*, rep from * to * 2x and * to ** 1x, dc in same sp as first dc, ch1, join with dc to first st.

R2

dc over joining dc, *dc in each st on side**, (dc, ch2, dc) in 2-ch cnr sp*, rep from * to * 2x and * to ** 1x, dc in same sp as first st, ch1, join with dc to first st.

R3

ch3 (stch), *tr in each st on side**, (tr, ch2, tr) in 2-ch cnr sp*, rep from * to * 2x and * to ** 1x, tr in same sp as first st, ch1, join with dc to 3rd ch of stch.

R4

dc over joining dc, *dc in each st on side**, (dc, ch2, dc) in 2-ch cnr sp*, rep from * to * 2x and * to ** 1x, dc in same sp as first st, ch1, join with dc to first st.

R5

dc over joining dc, *dc in each st on side**, (dc, ch2, dc) in 2-ch cnr sp*, rep from * to * 2x and * to ** 1x, dc in same sp as first st, ch2, join with ss to first st.
Fasten off.

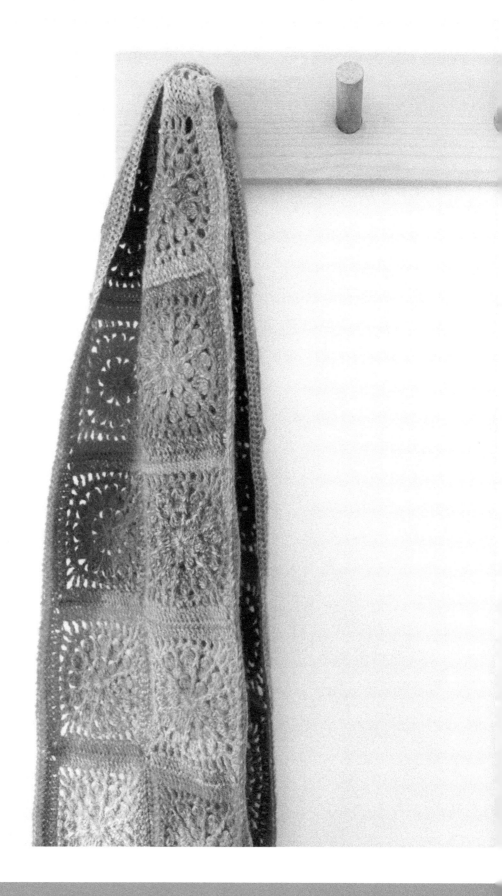

The Dahlia Scarf uses the Dahlia pattern on page 36, and a border of a round of dc followed by a round of tr. See this project on page 85.

Patterns

Deco : Page 22

Camellia : Page 23

Salish : Page 24

Happy Hexie : Page 26

Ianthe : Page 27

Arafura : Page 28

Crop Circles : Page 29

Rosette : Page 30

Clover : Page 31

Berry Flower : Page 32

Fhool : Page 34

Corona : Page 35

Dahlia : Page 36

Sharing : Page 37

Cirque : Page 38

Florence : Page 39

Anemone : Page 40

Framed : Page 42

Granny Flower : Page 43

D'Urville : Page 44

Killarney : Page 46

Ollie : Page 47

Iron Lace : Page 48

Solomon : Page 50

Kruis : Page 51

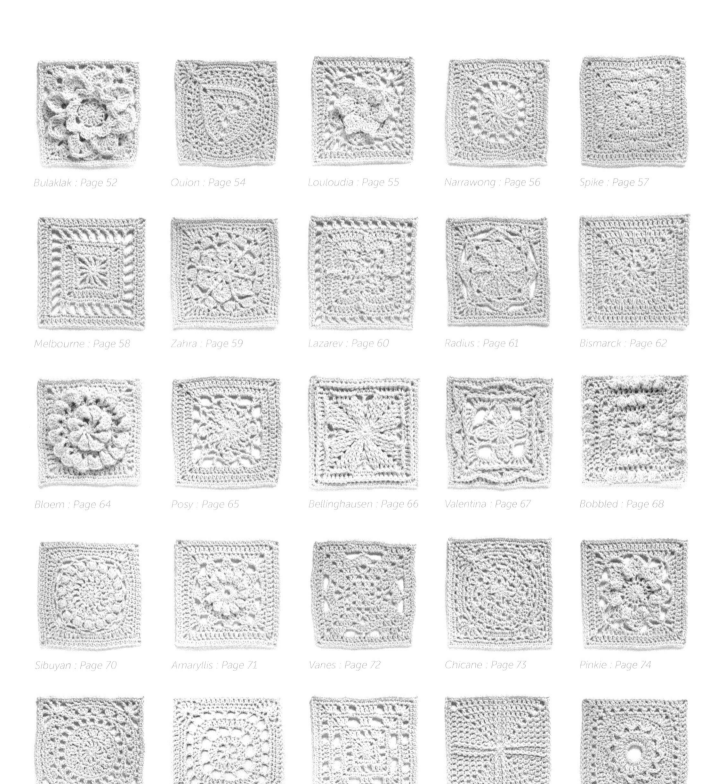

Bulaklak : Page 52

Quion : Page 54

Louloudia : Page 55

Narrawong : Page 56

Spike : Page 57

Melbourne : Page 58

Zahra : Page 59

Lazarev : Page 60

Radius : Page 61

Bismarck : Page 62

Bloem : Page 64

Posy : Page 65

Bellinghausen : Page 66

Valentina : Page 67

Bobbled : Page 68

Sibuyan : Page 70

Amaryllis : Page 71

Vanes : Page 72

Chicane : Page 73

Pinkie : Page 74

Mozambique : Page 75

Cogs : Page 76

Banda : Page 77

Traverse : Page 78

Sol : Page 79

Deco

  34m

Begin with mc.

R1: ch4 (stch), 15dtr, join with ss to 4th ch of stch. {16 sts}

R2: ch4 (stch), dtr in same st as ss, 2dtr in next 15 sts, join with ss to 4th ch of stch. {32 sts}

R3: ch4 (stch), dtr in same st as ss, *dtr in next st** 2dtr in next st*, rep from * to * 14x and * to ** 1x, join with ss to 4th ch of stch. {48 sts}

R4: ch4 (stch), dtr in same st as ss, *dtr in next 2 sts** 2dtr in next st*, rep from * to * 14x and * to ** 1x, join with ss to 4th ch of stch. {64 sts}

R5: ch4 (stch), tr in same st as ss, *bptr around next st, bphtr around next st, bpdc around next 11 sts, bphtr around next st, bptr around next st** (tr, dtr, ch2, dtr, tr) in next st*, rep from * to * 2x and * to ** 1x, (tr, dtr) in same st as first sts, ch1, join with dc to 4th ch of stch.
{19 sts on each side; 4 2-ch cnr sps}

R6: dc over joining dc, *dc in next 19 sts** (dc, ch2, dc) in 2-ch sp*, rep from * to * 2x and * to ** 1x, dc in same sp as first st, ch2, join with ss to first st. Fasten off.
{21 sts on each side; 4 2-ch cnr sps}

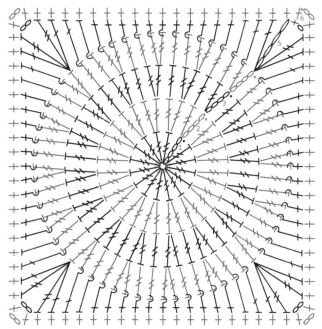

Cascade Ultra Pima
1-2 Turquoise 3733
3-4 Aqua 3732
5 Ice 3736
6 Natural 3718

Dedri's Deco
Scheepjes Catona
1 Yellow 208
2 Powder Pink 238
3 Tulip Pink 222
4 Dark Pink 114
5-6 Green Yellow 245
www.lookatwhatimade.net

Bendigo Woollen Mills
Cotton 8 ply
1-4 Glacier 818
5-6 Storm Cloud 827

Camellia

  42m

Attach yarn to hook with a slip knot, ch1, work all R1 sts into the 1-ch sp.

R1: ch3 (stch), *ch1, tr*, rep from * to * 6x, join with dc to 3rd ch of stch. {8 sts, 8 1-ch sps}

R2: dc over joining dc, *(htr, tr, htr) in next st**, dc in 1-ch sp*, rep from * to * 6x and * to ** 1x, join with ss to first st. {32 sts}

R3: *spike dc into 1-ch sp of R1 below**, ch3, skip 3 sts*, rep from * to * 6x and * to ** 1x, ch1, join with htr to first st. {8 sts, 8 3-ch sps}

R4: dc over joining htr, *(htr, 2tr, htr) in next st**, dc in 3-ch sp*, rep from * to * 6x and * to ** 1x, join with ss to first st. {40 sts}

R5: *spike dc into 3-ch sp of R3 below**, ch4, skip 4 sts*, rep from * to * 6x and * to ** 1x, ch1, join with tr to first st. {8 sts, 8 4-ch sps}

R6: dc over joining tr, *(htr, 3tr, htr) in next st**, dc in 4-ch sp*, rep from * to * 6x and * to ** 1x, join with ss to first st. {48 sts}

R7: *spike dc into 4-ch sp of R5 below**, ch5, skip 5 sts*, rep from * to * 6x and * to ** 1x, ch2, join with tr to first st. {8 sts, 8 5-ch sps}

R8: dc over joining tr, *(htr, 4tr, htr) in next st**, dc in 5-ch sp*, rep from * to * 6x and * to ** 1x, join with ss to first st. {56 sts}

R9: *spike dc into 5-ch sp of R7 below, ch6, skip 6 sts*, rep from * to * 7x, join with ss to first st. {8 sts, 8 6-ch sps}

R10: ch4 (stch), dtr in same st as ss, *(2hdtr, 2tr, 2htr, dc) in 6-ch sp, dc in next st, (dc, 2htr, 2tr, 2hdtr) in 6-ch sp**, 3dtr in next st*, rep from * to * 2x and * to ** 1x, dtr in same sp as first sts, join with ss to 4th ch of stch. {15 sts on each side; 4 3-st cnrs}

R11: ch3 (stch), *2x [tr in next st, htr in next 2 sts, dc in next 3 sts, htr in next 2 sts], tr in next st**, (tr, ch2, tr) in next st*, rep from * to * 2x and * to ** 1x, tr in same sp as first st, ch1, join with dc to 3rd ch of stch. {19 sts on each side; 4 2-ch cnr sps}

R12: dc over joining dc, *dc in next 19 sts**, (dc, ch2, dc) in next st*, rep from * to * 2x and * to ** 1x, dc in same sp as first st, ch1, join with dc to first st. {21 sts on each side; 4 2-ch cnr sps}

R13: dc over joining dc, *dc in next 21 sts**, (dc, ch2, dc) in next st*, rep from * to * 2x and * to ** 1x, dc in same sp as first st, ch2, join with ss to first st. Fasten off. {23 sts on each side; 4 2-ch cnr sps}

Bendigo Woollen Mills
Cotton 8 ply
1 Daffodil 806
2 Pink Rose 905
3-4 Blush 811
5-6 Pomegranate 819
7-9 Kiwi 809
10-13 French Navy 814

Cascade Ultra Pima
1-4 Turquoise 3733
5-8 Aqua 3732
9-10 Ice 3736
11-13 Natural 3718

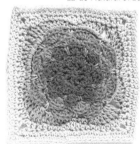

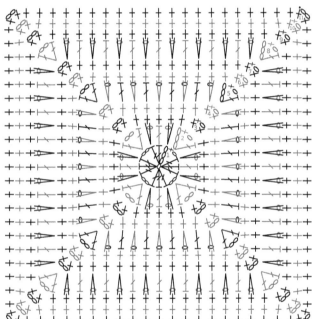

Salish

 36m

Attach yarn to hook with a slip knot, ch1, work all R1 sts into the 1-ch sp.

R1: ch3 (stch), 2tr, *ch2, 3tr*, rep from * to * 2x, ch1, join with dc to 3rd ch of stch. {3 sts on each side; 4 2-ch sps}

R2: ch3 (stch), *ch1, skip 1 st, tr in next st, ch1, skip 1 st**, (tr, ch2, tr) in 2-ch sp*, rep from * to * 2x and * to ** 1x, tr in same sp as first st, ch1, join with dc to 3rd ch of stch. {3 sts, 2 1-ch sps on each side; 4 2-ch cnr sps}

R3: dc over joining dc, *2x [dc in next st, spike dc in skipped st of R1 below], dc in next st**, (dc, ch2, dc) in 2-ch sp*, rep from * to * 2x and * to ** 1x, dc in same sp as first st, ch1, join with dc to first st. {7 sts on each side; 4 2-ch cnr sps}

R4: dc over joining dc, *dc in next 7 sts**, (dc, ch2, dc) in 2-ch sp*, rep from * to * 2x and * to ** 1x, dc in same sp as first st, ch1, join with dc to first st. {9 sts on each side; 4 2-ch cnr sps}

R5: ch3 (stch), *4x [ch1, skip 1 st, tr in next st], ch1, skip 1 st**, (tr, ch2, tr) in 2-ch sp*, rep from * to * 2x and * to ** 1x, tr in same sp as first st, ch1, join with dc to 3rd ch of stch. {6 sts, 5 1-ch sps on each side; 4 2-ch cnr sps}

R6: dc over joining dc, *5x [dc in next st, spike dc in skipped st of R4 below], dc in next st**, (dc, ch2, dc) in 2-ch sp*, rep from * to * 2x and * to ** 1x, dc in same sp as first st, ch1, join with dc to first st. {13 sts on each side; 4 2-ch cnr sps}

R7: dc over joining dc, *dc in next 13 sts**, (dc, ch2, dc) in 2-ch sp*, rep from * to * 2x and * to ** 1x, dc in same sp as first st, ch1, join with dc to first st. {15 sts on each side; 4 2-ch cnr sps}

R8: ch3 (stch), *7x [ch1, skip 1 st, tr in next st], ch1, skip 1 st**, (tr, ch2, tr) in 2-ch sp*, rep from * to * 2x and * to ** 1x, tr in same sp as first st, ch1, join with dc to 3rd ch of stch. {9 sts, 8 1-ch sps on each side; 4 2-ch cnr sps}

R9: dc over joining dc, *8x [dc in next st, spike dc in skipped st of R7 below], dc in next st**, (dc, ch2, dc) in 2-ch sp*, rep from * to * 2x and * to ** 1x, dc in same sp as first st, ch1, join with dc to first st.
{19 sts on each side; 4 2-ch cnr sps}

R10: dc over joining dc, *dc in next 19 sts**, (dc, ch2, dc) in 2-ch sp*, rep from * to * 2x and * to ** 1x, dc in same sp as first st, ch1, join with dc to first st.
{21 sts on each side; 4 2-ch cnr sps}

R11: dc over joining dc, *dc in next 21 sts**, (dc, ch2, dc) in next st*, rep from * to * 2x and * to ** 1x, dc in same sp as first st, ch2, join with ss to first st. Fasten off.
{23 sts on each side; 4 2-ch cnr sps}

To extend

Rep R8, R9 and R10 as many times as needed, increasing the numbers as follows:

R8 "#+3x [ch1, skip 1 ..." {#+3 sts, #+3 1-ch sps ...}

R9 "#+3x [dc in next st ... of R#+3 ..." {#+6 sts ...}

R10 "dc in next #+6 sts ..." {#+6 sts ...}

Bendigo Woollen Mills
Cotton 8 ply
1-2, 5 and 8 Blue Ice Crush
3, 6 and 9 Blueberry Crush
4, 7 and 10-11 Parchment

Paintbox Cotton DK
1-2 and 6-8 Banana Cream 421
3-5 and 9-11 Soft Fudge 410

Cascade Ultra Pima
1-2 Turquoise 3733
3-5 Aqua 3732
6-8 Ice 3736
9-11 Natural 3718

Happy Hexie

🧶 🧶 34m

R1: ch3 (stch), *ch2**, tr*, rep from * to * 4x and * to ** 1x, join with ss to 3rd ch of stch. {6 sts, 6 2-ch sps}

R2: ss to 2-ch sp, ch3 (stch), 2tr in same 2-ch sp, *ch2, skip 1 st**, 3tr in 2-ch sp*, rep from * to * 4x and * to ** 1x, ch1, join with dc to 3rd ch of stch.
{3 sts on each side; 6 2-ch cnr sps}

R3: dc over joining dc, *dc in next 3 sts**, (dc, ch2, dc) in 2-ch sp*, rep from * to * 4x and * to ** 1x, dc in same sp as first st, ch1, join with dc to first st.
{5 sts on each side; 6 2-ch cnr sps}

R4: ch3 (stch), *tr in next 5 sts**, (tr, ch1, tr) in 2-ch sp*, rep from * to * 4x and * to ** 1x, tr in same sp as first st, join with dc to 3rd ch of stch.
{7 sts on each side; 6 1-ch cnr sps}

R5: dc over joining dc, *dc in next 7 sts**, (dc, ch2, dc) in 1-ch sp*, rep from * to * 4x and * to ** 1x, dc in same sp as first st, ch1, join with dc to first st.
{9 sts on each side; 6 2-ch cnr sps}

R6: dc over joining dc, *4x [ch1, skip 1 st, tr in next st], ch1, skip 1 st**, dc in 2-ch sp*, rep from * to * 4x and * to ** 1x, join with ss to first st. {30 sts, 30 1-ch sps}

R7: dc in same st as ss, *dc in 1-ch sp**, dc in next st*, rep from * to * 28x and * to ** 1x, join with ss to first st. {60 sts}

R8: ch4 (stch), hdtr in same st as ss, *tr in next 2 sts, htr in next 3 sts, dc in next 4 sts, htr in next 3 sts, tr in next 2 sts**, (hdtr, dtr, ch2, dtr, hdtr) in next st*, rep from * to * 2x and * to ** 1x, (hdtr, dtr) in same st as first sts, ch1, join with dc to 4th ch of stch. {18 sts on each side; 4 2-ch cnr sps}

R9: ch2 (stch), *3x [ch1, skip 1 st, htr in next st], ch1, skip 1 st, htr in next 4 sts, 3x [ch1, skip 1 st, htr in next st], ch1, skip 1 st**, (htr, ch2, htr) in 2-ch sp*, rep from * to * 2x and * to ** 1x, htr in same sp as first st, ch1, join with dc to 2nd ch of stch. {12 sts, 8 1-ch sps on each side; 4 2-ch cnr sps}

R10: dc over joining dc, *4x [dc in next st, dc in 1-ch sp], dc in next 4 sts, 4x [dc in 1-ch sp, dc in next st]**, (dc, ch2, dc) in 2-ch sp*, rep from * to * 2x and * to ** 1x, dc in same sp as first st, ch2, join with ss to first st.
{22 sts on each side; 4 2-ch cnr sps}

Cascade Ultra Pima
1-3 Turquoise 3733
4-5 Aqua 3732
6-8 Ice 3736
9-10 Natural 3718

Tarndie Polwarth 100% Natural
1-5 White
6-7 Taupe
8-10 Dark

Ianthe

  40m

Begin with a mc or ch4 and join the last ch to the first with a ss to make a loop.

R1: ch3 (stch), *ch2, 3trcl, ch2**, tr, ch2, tr*, rep from * to * 2x and * to ** 1x, tr, ch1, join with dc for 3rd ch of stch. {3 sts, 2 2-ch sps on each side; 4 2-ch cnr sps}

R2: ch3 (stch), *tr in next st, tr in 2-ch sp, fptr around next st, tr in 2-ch sp, tr in next st**, (tr, ch2, tr) in 2-ch sp*, rep from * to * 2x and * to ** 1x, tr in same sp as first st, ch1, join with dc to 3rd ch of stch. {7 sts on each side; 4 2-ch cnr sps}

R3: dc over joining dc, *dc in next 3 sts, fptr around next st, dc in next 3 sts**, (dc, ch2, dc) in 2-ch sp*, rep from * to * 2x and * to ** 1x, dc in same sp as first st, ch1, join with dc to first st. {9 sts on each side; 4 2-ch cnr sps}

R4: ch3 (stch), *tr in next 2 sts, 3trcl in next st, tr in next st, fptr around next st, tr in next st, 3trcl in next st, tr in next 2 sts**, (tr, ch2, tr) in 2-ch sp*, rep from * to * 2x and * to ** 1x, tr in same sp as first st, ch1, join with dc to 3rd ch of stch. {11 sts on each side; 4 2-ch cnr sps}

R5: ch3 (stch), *tr in next 3 sts, 2x [fptr around next st, tr in next st], fptr around next st, tr in next 3 sts**, (tr, ch2, tr) in 2-ch sp*, rep from * to * 2x and * to ** 1x, tr in same sp as first st, ch1, join with dc to 3rd ch of stch. {13 sts on each side; 4 2-ch cnr sps}

R6: dc over joining dc, *dc in next 4 sts, 2x [fptr around next st, dc in next st], fptr around next st, dc in next 4 sts**, (dc, ch2, dc) in 2-ch sp*, rep from * to * 2x and * to ** 1x, dc in same sp as first st, ch1, join with dc to first st. {15 sts on each side; 4 2-ch cnr sps}

R7: ch3 (stch), *tr in next 3 sts, 3trcl in next st, 3x [tr in next st, fptr around next st], tr in next st, 3trcl in next st, tr in next 3 sts**, (tr, ch2, tr) in 2-ch sp*, rep from * to * 2x and * to ** 1x, tr in same sp as first st, ch1, join with dc to 3rd ch of stch. {17 sts on each side; 4 2-ch cnr sps}

R8. dc over joining dc, *dc in next 4 sts, 4x [fptr around next st, dc in next st], fptr around next st, dc in next 4 sts**, (dc, ch2, dc) in 2-ch sp*, rep from * to * 2x and * to ** 1x, dc in same sp as first st, ch1, join with dc to first st. {19 sts on each side; 4 2-ch cnr sps}

R9: dc over joining dc, *dc in next 19 sts**, (dc, ch2, dc) in 2-ch sp*, rep from * to * 2x and * to ** 1x, dc in same sp as first st, ch2, join with ss to first st. Fasten off. {21 sts on each side; 4 2-ch cnr sps}

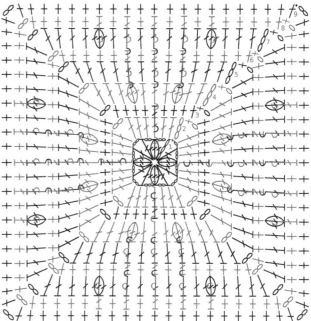

Bendigo Woollen Mills
Cotton 8 ply
1 and 5-7 Pink Rose 805
2-4 and 8-9 Kiwi 809

Cascade Ultra Pima
1-3 Turquoise 3733
4-6 Aqua 3732
7-8 Ice 3736
9 Natural 3718

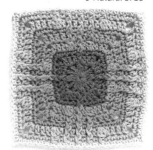

Arafura

  30m

Begin with a mc or ch4 and join the last ch to the first with a ss to make a loop.

R1: ch3 (stch), 15tr, join with ss to 3rd ch of stch. {16 sts}

R2: ch3 (stch), tr in previous st, *tr in next st, tr in previous st*, rep from * to * 14x, join with ss to 3rd ch of stch. {32 sts}

R3: ch4 (stch), dtr in next st, *ch3, dc in next 4 sts, ch3**, dtr in next 4 sts*, rep from * to * 2x and * to ** 1x, dtr in next 2 sts, join with ss to 4th ch of stch. {32 sts, 8 3-ch sps}

R4: ch4 (stch), dtr in next st, *dtr in 3-ch sp, ch4, dc in next 4 sts, ch4, dtr in 3-ch sp**, dtr in next 4 sts*, rep from * to * 2x and * to ** 1x, dtr in next 2 sts, join with ss to 4th ch of stch. {40 sts, 8 4-ch sps}

R5: dc in same st as ss, dc in next 2 sts, *ch3, skip 4-ch sp, dtr in blo of next 4 sts, ch3, skip 4-ch sp, dc in next 3 sts**, ch2, dc in next 3 sts*, rep from * to * 2x and * to ** 1x, ch1, join with dc to first st. {10 sts, 2 3-ch sps on each side; 4 2-ch cnr sps}

R6: ch3 (stch), tr over joining dc, *tr in blo of next 3 sts, tr in each of the next 3 ch, tr in blo of next 4 sts, tr in each of the next 3 ch, tr in blo of next 3 sts**, (2tr, ch2, 2tr) in 2-ch sp*, rep from * to * 2x and * to ** 1x, 2tr in same sp as first sts, ch1, join with dc to 3rd ch of stch. {20 sts on each side; 4 2-ch cnr sps}

R7: dc over joining dc, *dc in next 20 sts**, (dc, ch2, dc) in 2-ch sp*, rep from * to * 2x and * to ** 1x, dc in same sp as first st, ch2, join with ss to first st. Fasten off. {22 sts on each side; 4 2-ch cnr sps}

Cascade Ultra Pima
1-2 Turquoise 3733
3-4 Aqua 3732
5 Ice 3736
6-7 Natural 3718

Great Ocean Road Woollen Mill
Loch Ard
1-4 Granite
5-7 Riverstone

Bendigo Woollen Mills
Cotton 4 ply
1-2, 5 and 7 Arctic 808
3-4 and 6 French Navy 814

Crop Circles

Make 1 lge circle for the centre.
Attach yarn to hook with a slip knot, ch1, work all R1 sts into the 1-ch sp.

R1: ch3 (stch), 11tr, join with ss to 3rd ch of stch. {12 sts}

R2: ch3 (stch), tr in same st as ss, 2tr in each tr, join with ss to 3rd ch of stch. {24 sts}

R3: ch2 (stch), htr in same st as ss, *htr in next st**, 2htr in next st*, rep from * to * 10x and * to ** 1x, join with inv join to first htr. Fasten off. {36 sts}

Make 4 sml circles following R1 and R2 above. Do not cut yarn. Flip 1 sml circle over and place on lge circle right sides facing. Join together with a ss. Fasten off and weave in end to secure. Rep for remaining 3 sml circles, skipping 8 sts between each ss join on the lge circle.

R4: Join yarn with stdg dc to a sml circle in lbv of st opposite ss join to lge circle, with 11 sts between the ss join and stdg dc, *dc in lbv of next 3 sts, htr in lbv of next st, tr in lbv of next 5 sts, skip (2 sts on sml circle, ss join and 3 sts on lge circle), dc in lbv of next 2 sts of lge circle, skip (3 sts on lge circle, ss join and 2 sts on sml circle), tr in lbv of next 5 sts, htr in lbv of next st, dc in lbv of next 3 sts**, (dc, ch2, dc) in lbv of next st*, rep from * to * 2x and * to ** 1x, dc in lbv of same st as first st, ch1, join with dc to first st. {22 sts on each side; 4 2-ch cnr sps}

R5: dc over joining dc, *dc in next 3 sts, htr in next 3 sts, tr in next st, hdtr in next st, dtr in next st, skip 4 sts, dtr in next st, hdtr in next st, tr in next st, htr in next 3 sts, dc in next 3 sts**, (dc, ch2, dc) in 2-ch sp*, rep from * to * 2x and * to ** 1x, dc in same sp as first st, ch1, join with dc to first st. {20 sts on each side; 4 2-ch cnr sps}

R6: dc over joining dc, *dc in next 9 sts, htr in next 2 sts, dc in next 9 sts**, (dc, ch2, dc) in 2-ch sp*, rep from * to * 2x and * to ** 1x, dc in same sp as first st, ch2, join with ss to first st. Fasten off. {22 sts on each side; 4 2-ch sps}

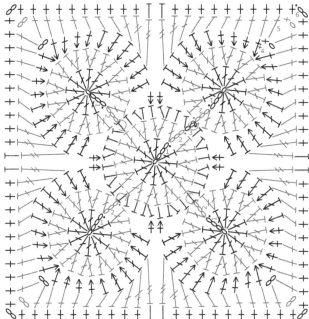

Pony's Crop Circles, Patons Cotton Blend
Lge circle: 1 Black 02
2 Pineapple 40
3 Wild Rose 39
Sml circles: 1 Persian Green 30
2 Natural 3718 04
4-5 Black 02
6 Cloud 34
www.instagram.com/ponymctate/

Cascade Ultra Pima
Lge circle: Turquoise 3733
Sml circles: Aqua 3732
4 Ice 3736
5-6 Natural 3718

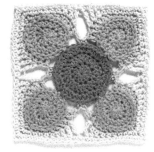

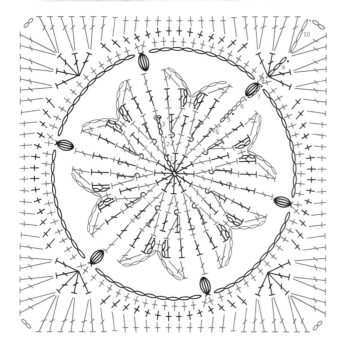

Rosette

  38m

NOTES

- R3: do not work a false tr at the start.
- R7: the ch3 (stch) and 4trpc equal 1 pc.

Attach yarn to hook with a slip knot, ch1, work all R1 sts into the 1-ch sp.

R1: ch3 (stch), 11tr, join with ss to 3rd ch of stch. {12 sts}

R2: ch3 (stch), tr in same st as ss, 2tr in next 11 sts, join with ss to 3rd ch of stch. {24 sts}

R3: ch3 (stch), *fptr around next st**, tr in next st*, rep from * to * 10x and * to ** 1x, join with inv join to first fp st. {24 sts}

R4: Attach with a stdg bpdc around a tr (not a fptr), *2tr in R2 st behind fp st of R3, skip 1 st, 2tr in R2 st behind fp st of R3**, bpdc around next st*, rep from * to * 4x and * to ** 1x, join with ss to first st. {30 sts}

R5: ch3 (stch), tr in next st, *(tr, ch2, ss) in next st, (ss, ch2, tr) in next st**, tr in next 3 sts*, rep from * to * 4x and * to ** 1x, tr in next st, join with ss to 3rd ch of stch. {42 sts, 12 2-ch sps}

R6: ch3 (stch), *tr2tog over next 2 sts, ch4, skip 2-ch sp, dc in gap between R4 sts below, ch4, skip 2-ch sp, tr2tog over next 2 sts**, tr in next st*, rep from * to * 4x and * to ** 1x, join with ss to 3rd ch of stch. {24 sts, 12 4-ch sps}

R7: ch3, 4trpc in same st as ss, *ch10, skip (1 st, 4-ch sp, 1 st, 4-ch sp and 1 st)**, pc in next st*, rep from * to * 4x and * to ** 1x, join with ss to top of 4trpc. {6 sts, 6 10-ch sps}

R8: dc in same st as ss, *12dc in 10-ch sp**, 2dc in pc*, rep from * to * 4x and * to ** 1x, dc in same st as first st, join with ss to first st. {84 sts}

R9: ch3 (stch), 2tr in same st as ss, *skip 3 sts, dc in next 14 sts, skip 3 sts**, 5tr in next st*, rep from * to * 2x and * to ** 1x, 2tr in same st as first sts, join with ss to 3rd ch of stch. {14 sts on each side; 4 5-st cnrs}

R10: ch3 (stch), tr in same st as ss, *2tr in next 2 sts, tr in next st, htr in next st, dc in next 10 sts, htr in next st, tr in next st, 2tr in next 2 sts**, (2tr, ch2, 2tr) in next st*, rep from * to * 2x and * to ** 1x, 2tr in same st as first sts, ch2, join with ss to 3rd ch of stch. Fasten off. {26 sts on each side; 4 2-ch cnr sps}

Cascade Ultra Pima
1-3 Turquoise 3733
4-7 Aqua 3732
8-9 Ice 3736
10 Natural 3718

Scheepjes Catona
1-3 Tangerine 281
4-7 Yellow Gold 208
8-10 Kiwi 205

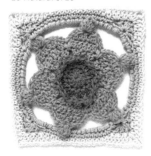 

Clover

   32m

Begin with a mc or ch4 and join the last ch to the first with a ss to make a loop.

R1: ch3 (stch), tr, *ch2, 2tr* rep from * to * 6x, ch1, join with dc to 3rd ch of stch. {16 sts, 8 2-ch sps}

R2: ch3 (stch), 2tr over joining dc, *skip 2 sts, dc in 2-ch sp, skip 2 sts**, (3tr, ch2, 3tr) in 2-ch sp*, rep from * to * 2x and * to ** 1x, 3tr in same sp as first sts, ch1, join with dc to 3rd ch of stch. {7 sts on each side; 4 2-ch cnr sps}

R3: (dc, ch4, dc) over joining dc, *dc in next 3 sts, ch4, skip 1 st, dc in next 3 sts**, (dc, ch4, dc, ch4, dc) in 2-ch sp*, rep from * to * 2x and * to ** 1x, (dc, ch4) in same sp as first sts, join with ss to first st.
{8 sts, 3 4-ch sps on each side; 4 1-st cnrs}

R4: dc in same sp as ss, *5dc in 4-ch sp, skip 2 sts, dc in next st, skip 1 st, 5dc in 4-ch sp, skip 1 st, dc in next st, skip 2 sts, 5dc in 4-ch sp**, dc in next st*, rep from * to * 2x and * to ** 1x, join with ss to first st.
{17 sts on each side; 4 1-st cnrs}

R5: ch4 (stch), *ch4, skip 2 sts, htr in next st, ch3, skip 5 sts, dc in next st, ch3, skip 5 sts, htr in next st, ch4, skip 2 sts**, (dtr, ch3, dtr) in next st*, rep from * to * 2x and * to ** 1x, dtr in same sp as first st, ch1, join with htr to 4th ch of stch.
{5 sts, 2 4-ch sps, 2 3-ch sps on each side; 4 3-ch cnr sps}

R6: 2dc over joining htr, *dc in next st, 3dc in 4-ch sp, 2x [dc in next st, 3dc in 3-ch sp], dc in next st, 3dc in 4-ch sp, dc in next st**, (2dc, ch2, 2dc) in 3-ch sp*, rep from * to * 2x and * to ** 1x, 2dc in same sp as first sts, ch1, join with dc to first st. {21 sts on each side; 4 2-ch cnr sps}

R7: ch2 (stch), *2x [ch2, skip 2 sts, htr in next 2 sts], ch2, skip 1 st, htr3tog over next 3 sts, ch2, skip 1 st, 2x [htr in next 2 sts, ch2, skip 2 sts]**, (htr, ch2, htr) in 2-ch sp*, rep from * to * 2x and * to ** 1x, htr in same sp as first st, ch1, join with dc to 2nd ch of stch.
{11 sts, 6 2-ch sps on each side; 4 2-ch cnr sps}

R8: dc over joining dc, *dc in next st, 2x [2dc in 2-ch sp, dc in next 2 sts], 2dc in 2-ch sp, dc in next st, 2x [2dc in 2-ch sp, dc in next 2 sts], 2dc in 2-ch sp, dc in next st**, (dc, ch2, dc) in 2-ch sp*, rep from * to * 2x and * to ** 1x, dc in same sp as first st, ch2, join with ss to first st. Fasten off.
{25 sts on each side; 4 2-ch cnr sps}

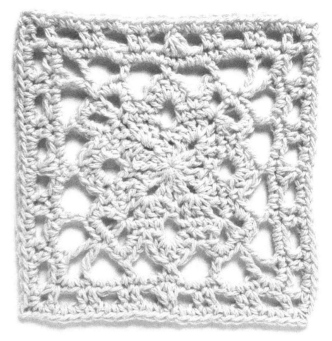

Bendigo Woollen Mills
Cotton 8 ply
1-4 Kiwi 809
5-8 Latte 887

Cascade Ultra Pima
1-2 Turquoise 3733
3-4 Aqua 3732
5-6 Ice 3736
7-8 Natural 3718

Berry Flower

  47m

NOTES

- R1: the ch1 at the start is not included in the st count.
- R2 and R3: do not use a false st at the start; the ch sps at the start of these rounds are included in the st counts.
- R8: the ch3 (stch) and tr4tog count as 1 tr5tog.

Begin with a mc or ch4 and join the last ch to the first with a ss to make a loop.

R1: ch1, 20dc, join with ss to first st. {20 sts}

R2: *ch3, 2dtr in next st, (2dtr, ch3, ss) in next st, dc in next st**, ss in next st*, rep from * to * 3x and * to ** 1x, do not join. {35 sts, 10 3-ch sps}

R3: *ch4, skip (ss, 3-ch sp, 4 sts, 3-ch sp and ss)**, dc in next st*, rep from * to * 3x and * to ** 1x, join with ss to last st of R2. {5 sts, 5 4-ch sps}

R4: dc in same st as ss, *(ss, ch3, 5dtr, ch3, ss) in 4-ch sp**, dc in next st*, rep from * to * 3x and * to ** 1x, join with ss to first st. {40 sts, 10 3-ch sps}

R5: dc in same st as ss, *ch5, skip (ss, 3-ch sp, 5 sts, 3-ch sp and ss)**, dc in next st*, rep from * to * 3x and * to ** 1x, join with ss to first st. {5 sts, 5 5-ch sps}

R6: dc in same st as ss, *(ss, ch3, 6dtr, ch3, ss) in 5-ch sp**, dc in next st*, rep from * to * 3x and * to ** 1x, join with ss to first st. {45 sts, 10 3-ch sps}

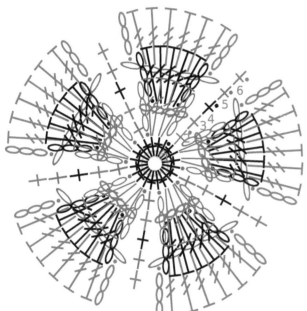

R7: ch4 (stch), 4dtr in same st as ss, *ch5, skip (ss, 3-ch sp, 6 sts, 3-ch sp and ss)**, 5dtr in next st*, rep from * to * 3x and * to ** 1x, join with ss to 4th ch of stch. {25 sts, 5 5-ch sps}

R8: ch3 (stch), tr4tog over next 4 sts, *ch3, 5dc in 5-ch sp, ch3**, tr5tog over next 5 sts*, rep from * to * 3x and * to ** 1x, join with ss to tr4tog. {30 sts, 10 3-ch sps}

R9: *fpdc around st below, ch4, skip 3-ch sp, tr in next 5 sts, ch4, skip 3-ch sp*, rep from * to * 4x, join with ss to first st. {30 sts, 10 4-ch sps}

R10: dc in same st as ss, *4dc in 4-ch sp, dc in next 2 sts, 2dc in next st, dc in next 2 sts, 4dc in 4-ch sp**, 2dc in next st*, rep from * to * 3x and from * to ** once, dc in same st as first st, join with ss to first st. {80 sts}

R11: ch4 (stch), 3dtr in same st as ss, *skip 3 sts, dc in next 13 sts, skip 3 sts**, 7dtr in next st*, rep from * to * 2x and from * to ** 1x, 3dtr in same st as first st, join with ss to 4th ch of stch. {13 sts on each side; 4 7-st cnrs}

R12: dc in same st as ss, *dc in next 3 sts, htr in next st, dc in next 11 sts, htr in next st, dc in next 3 sts**, (dc, ch2, dc) in next st*, rep from * to * 2x and from * to ** 1x, dc in same sp as first st, ch1, join with dc to first dc. {21 sts on each side; 4 2-ch cnr sps}

R13: dc over joining dc, *dc in next 21 sts**, (dc, ch2, dc) in 2-ch sp*, rep from * to * 2x and from * to ** 1x, dc in same sp as first st, ch2, join with ss to first dc. Fasten off. {23 sts on each side; 4 2-ch cnr sps}

Paintbox Cotton DK
1 Buttercup Yellow 423
2-3 Tomato Red 413
4-5 Pillar Red 415
6 Red Wine 416
7-8 Evergreen 431
9-13 Marine Blue 434

Robyn's Berry Flower
KPC Yarn Gossyp Cotton
1-3, 6-8 and 12-13 Ballerina
4-5 and 9-11 Rosie
www.yummyyarnandco.com.au

Cascade Ultra Pima
1-4 Turquoise 3733
5-6 Aqua 3732
7-8 Ice 3736
9-13 Natural 3718

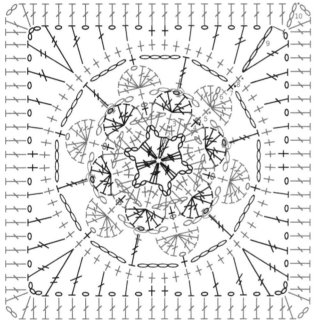

Fhool

  36m

Begin with a mc or ch4 and join the last ch to the first with a ss to make a loop.

R1: ch3 (stch), tr, *ch4, 3tr*, rep from * to * 4x, ch4, tr, join with ss to 3rd ch of stch. {18 sts, 6 4-ch sps}

R2: dc in same st as ss, *skip 1 st, (dc, htr, tr, ch1, tr, htr, dc) in 4-ch sp, skip 1 st**, dc in next st*, rep from * to * 4x and * to ** 1x, join with ss to first st. {42 sts, 6 1-ch sps}

R3: dc in same st as ss, *ch4, skip (3 sts, 1-ch sp and 3 sts)**, dc in next st*, rep from * to * 4x, ch1, join with tr to first st. {6 sts, 6 4-ch sps}

R4: dc over joining tr, *(3tr, ch1, 3tr) in next st**, dc in 4-ch sp*, rep from * to * 4x and * to ** 1x, join with ss to first st. {42 sts, 6 1-ch sps}

R5: dc in same st as ss, *ch5, skip (3 sts, 1-ch sp and 3 sts)**, dc in next st*, rep from * to * 4x and * to ** 1x, join with ss to first st. {6 sts, 6 5-ch sps}

R6: ch3 (stch), 3tr in same st as ss, *dc in 5-ch sp**, (4tr, ch1, 4tr) in next st*, rep from * to * 4x and * to ** 1x, 4tr in same sp as first sts, join with dc to 3rd ch of stch. {54 sts, 6 1-ch sps}

R7: dc over joining dc, *ch4, dtr in 1-ch sp of R4 below, ch4**, dc in 1-ch sp of R6*, rep from * to * 4x and * to ** 1x, join with ss to first st. {12 sts, 12 4-ch sps}

R8: dc in same st as ss, *4dc in 4-ch sp**, dc in next st*, rep from * to * 10x and * to ** 1x, join with ss to first st. {60 sts}

R9: ch4 (stch), *ch1, hdtr in next st, ch1, skip 1 st, tr in next st, ch1, skip 1 st, htr in next st, ch1, skip 1 st, dc in next 2 sts, ch1, skip 1 st, htr in next st, ch1, skip 1 st, tr in next st, ch1, skip 1 st, hdtr in next st, ch1**, (dtr, ch3, dtr) in next st*, rep from * to * 2x and * to ** 1x, dtr in same sp as first st, ch1, join with htr to 4th ch of stch. {10 sts, 8 1-ch sps on each side; 4 3-ch cnr sps}

R10: ch3 (stch), tr over joining htr, *4x [tr in next st, tr in 1-ch sp], tr in next 2 sts, 4x [tr in 1-ch sp, tr in next st]**, (2tr, ch2, 2tr) in 3-ch sp*, rep from * to * 2x and * to ** 1x, 2tr in same sp as first sts, ch2, join with ss to 3rd ch of stch. Fasten off. {22 sts on each side; 4 2-ch cnr sps}

Cascade Ultra Pima
1-5 Turquoise 3733
6 Aqua 3732
7-8 Ice 3736
9-10 Natural 3718

Paintbox Cotton DK
1 Banana Cream 421
2-3 Pale Lilac 446
4-5 Rich Mauve 445
6 Grass Green 430
7-10 Evergreen 431

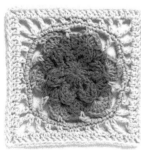 

Corona

 33m

Begin with a mc or ch4 and join the last ch to the first with a ss to make a loop.

R1: ch3 (stch), 15tr, join with ss to 3rd ch of stch. {16 sts}

R2: dc in same st as ss, *ch2, skip 1 st**, dc in next st*, rep from * to * 6x and * to ** 1x, join with ss to first st. {8 sts, 8 2-ch sps}

R3: ch3 (stch), *3tr in 2-ch sp**, tr in next st*, rep from * to * 6x and * to ** 1x, join with ss to 3rd ch of stch. {32 sts}

R4: dc in same st as ss, *ch2, skip 1 st**, dc in next st*, rep from * to * 14x and * to ** 1x, join with ss to first st. {16 sts, 16 2-ch sps}

R5: ch3 (stch), *3tr in 2-ch sp**, tr in next st*, rep from * to * 14x and * to ** 1x, join with ss to 3rd ch of stch. {64 sts}

R6: dc in same st as ss, *ch2, skip 1 st**, dc in next st*, rep from * to * 30x and * to ** 1x, join with ss to first st. {32 sts, 32 2-ch sps}

R7: ch4 (stch), hdtr in same st as ss, *tr in 2-ch sp, tr in next st, tr in 2-ch sp, htr in next st, htr in 2-ch sp, htr in next st, dc in 2-ch sp, dc in next st, dc in 2-ch sp, htr in next st, htr in 2-ch sp, htr in next st, tr in 2-ch sp, tr in next st, tr in 2-ch sp**, (hdtr, dtr, ch2, dtr, hdtr) in next st*, rep from * to * 2x and * to ** 1x, (hdtr, dtr) in same st as first sts, ch1, join with dc to 4th ch of stch. {19 sts on each side; 4 2-ch cnr sps}

R8: dc over joining dc, *9x [ch1, skip 1 st, dc in next st], ch1, skip 1 st**, (dc, ch2, dc) in 2-ch sp*, rep from * to * 2x and * to ** 1x, dc in same sp as first st, ch1, join with dc to first st. {11 sts, 10 1-ch sps sts on each side; 4 2-ch cnr sps}

R9: ch3 (stch), *10x [tr in next st, tr in 1-ch sp], tr in next st**, (tr, ch2, tr) in 2-ch sp*, rep from * to * 2x and * to ** 1x, tr in same sp as first st, ch2, join with ss to 3rd ch of stch. Fasten off. {23 sts on each side; 4 2-ch cnr sps}

Paintbox Cotton DK
1-2 Melon Sorbet 417
3-4 Soft Fudge 410
5 Coffee Bean 411
6-7 Grass Green 430
8-9 Evergreen 431

Cascade Ultra Pima
1-2 Turquoise 3733
3-4 Aqua 3732
5-6 Ice 3736
7-9 Natural 3718

King Cole Cottonsoft
1-5 Orchid 3033
6-9 Lime 1601

  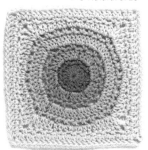

Dahlia

 33m

Begin with a mc or ch6 and join the last ch to the first with a ss to make a loop.

R1: ch3 (stch), 23tr, join with ss to 3rd ch of stch. Pull mc closed to 1 cm opening. {24 sts}

R2: fptr around st ss'd into, *ch2, tr3tog over next 3 sts, ch2**, fptr around next st*, rep from * to * 4x and * to ** 1x, join with ss to first st. {12 sts, 12 2-ch sps}

R3: fptr around st ss'd into, *3tr in 2-ch sp**, fptr around next st*, rep from * to * 10x and * to ** 1x, join with ss to first st. {48 sts}

R4: fptr around st ss'd into, *ch2, tr3tog over next 3 sts, ch2**, fptr around next st*, rep from * to * 10x and * to ** 1x, join with ss to first st. {24 sts, 24 2-ch sps}

R5: fpdc around st ss'd into, *2dc in 2-ch sp**, fpdc around next st*, rep from * to * 22x and * to ** 1x, join with ss to first st. {72 sts}

R6: ch4 (stch), *2x [ch1, skip 1 st, tr in next st], 4x [ch1, skip 1 st, htr in next st], 2x [ch1, skip 1 st, tr in next st], ch1, skip 1 st**, (dtr, ch3, dtr) in next st*, rep from * to * 2x and * to ** 1x, dtr in same sp as first st, ch1, join with htr to 4th ch of stch. {10 sts, 9 1-ch sps on each side; 4 3-ch cnr sps}

R7: ch3 (stch), tr over joining htr, *9x [tr in next st, tr in 1-ch sp], tr in next st**, (2tr, ch2, 2tr) in 3-ch sp*, rep from * to * 2x and * to ** 1x, 2tr in same sp as first sts, ch2, join with ss to 3rd ch of stch. Fasten off.
{23 sts on each side; 4 2-ch cnr sps}

Cascade Ultra Pima
1-2 Turquoise 3733
3-5 Aqua 3732
6 Ice 3736
7 Natural 3718

Bendigo Woollen Mills
Luxury 8 ply
1-2 Tangerine 347
3-4 Sunrise 336
5-7 Blue Denim 363

Paintbox Cotton DK
1-2 Rich Mauve 445
3-5 Banana Cream 421
6-7 Tomato Red 413

Sharing

 36m

NOTES

- **R2:** the ch3 (stch) and the 2trcl count as 1 3trcl.

Attach yarn to hook with a slip knot, ch1, work all R1 sts into the 1-ch sp.

R1: ch3 (stch), tr, *ch1, 2tr*, rep from * to * 4x, join with dc to 3rd ch of stch. {12 sts, 6 1-ch sps}

R2: ch3 (stch), 2trcl over joining dc, *ch1, skip 2 sts, (3trcl, ch1, 3trcl) in 1-ch sp*, rep from * to * 4x, 3trcl in same sp as first sts, join with dc to 2trcl. {12 sts, 12 1-ch sps}

R3: ch3 (stch), 2tr over joining dc, *ch1, skip 1 st, 3tr in 1-ch sp*, rep from * to * 10x, join with dc to 3rd ch of stch. {36 sts, 12 1-ch sps}

R4: dc over joining dc, *dc in next 3 sts, dc in 1-ch sp*, rep from * to * 10x, dc in next 3 sts, join with ss to first st. {48 sts}

R5: ch4 (stch), hdtr in same st as ss, *tr in next 2 sts, htr in next 2 sts, dc in next 3 sts, htr in next 2 sts, tr in next 2 sts**, (hdtr, dtr, ch2, dtr, hdtr) in next st*, rep from * to * 2x and * to ** 1x, (hdtr, dtr) in same st as first sts, ch1, join with dc to 4th ch of stch. {15 sts on each side; 4 2-ch cnr sps}

R6: dc over joining dc, *dc in next 15 sts**, (dc, ch2, dc) in 2-ch sp*, rep from * to * 2x and * to ** 1x, dc in same sp as first st, ch1, join with dc to first st. {17 sts on each side; 4 2-ch cnr sps}

R7: ch3 (stch), *8x [ch1, skip 1 st, tr in next st], ch1, skip 1 st**, (tr, ch3, tr) in 2-ch sp*, rep from * to* 2x and * to ** 1x, tr in same sp as first st, ch2, join with htr to 3rd ch of stch. {10 sts, 9 1-ch sps on each side; 4 3-ch cnr sps}

R8: 2dc over joining htr, *9x [dc in next st, dc in 1-ch sp], dc in next st**, (2dc, ch2, 2dc) in 3-ch sp*, rep from * to * 2x and * to ** 1x, 2dc in same sp as first sts, ch1, join with dc to first st. {23 sts on each side; 4 2-ch cnr sps}

R9: dc over joining dc, *dc in next 23 sts**, (dc, ch2, dc) in 2-ch sp*, rep from * to * 2x and * to ** 1x, dc in same sp as first st, ch2, join with ss to first st. Fasten off. {25 sts on each side; 4 2-ch cnr sps}

Scheepjes Catona
1 Hot Red 115
2 Yellow Gold 208
3-4 Kiwi 205
5-6 Vivid Blue 146
7-9 Electric Blue 201

Cascade Ultra Pima
1-3 Turquoise 3733
4-6 Aqua 3732
7 Ice 3736
8-9 Natural 3718

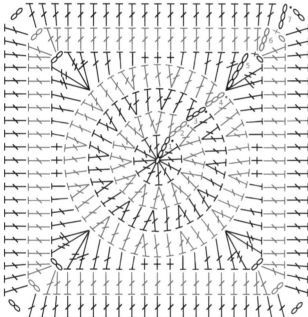

Cirque

  34m

NOTES

• R6 and R7: the corners are different.

Attach yarn to hook with a slip knot, ch1, work all R1 sts into the 1-ch sp.

R1: ch3 (stch), 11tr, join with ss to 3rd ch of stch. {12 sts}

R2: ch3 (stch), tr in same st as ss, 2tr in next 11 sts, join with ss to 3rd ch of stch. {24 sts}

R3: ch3 (stch), tr in same st as ss, *tr in next st, 2tr in next st*, rep from * to * 10x, tr in next st, join with ss to 3rd ch of stch. {36 sts}

R4: ch3 (stch), tr in same st as ss, *tr in next 2 sts**, 2tr in next st*, rep from * to * 10x and * to ** 1x, join with ss to 3rd ch of stch. {48 sts}

R5: ch4 (stch), hdtr in same st as ss, *tr in next 2 sts, htr in next 2 sts, dc in next 3 sts, htr in next 2 sts, tr in next 2 sts**, (hdtr, dtr, ch2, dtr, hdtr) in next st*, rep from * to * 2x and * to ** 1x, (hdtr, dtr) in same sp as first sts, ch1, join with dc to 4th ch of stch. {15 sts on each side; 4 2-ch cnr sps}

R6: ch3 (stch), tr over joining dc, *tr in next 15 sts**, (2tr, ch2, 2tr) in 2-ch sp*, rep from * to * 2x and * to ** 1x, 2tr in same sp as first sts, ch1, join with dc to 3rd ch of stch. {19 sts on each side; 4 2-ch cnr sps}

R7: ch3 (stch), *tr in next 19 sts**, (tr, ch2, tr) in 2-ch sp*, rep from * to * 2x and * to ** 1x, tr in same sp as first st, ch2, join with ss to 3rd ch of stch. Fasten off. {21 sts on each side; 4 2-ch cnr sps}

Cascade Ultra Pima
1-2 Turquoise 3733
3-4 Aqua 3732
5 Ice 3736
6-7 Natural 3718

Paintbox Cotton DK
1 Rich Mauve 445
2 Royal Blue 441
3 Marine Blue 434
4 Grass Green 430
5 Buttercup Yellow 423
6 Blood Orange 420
7 Pillar Red 415

Bendigo Woollen Mills
Cotton 4 ply
1-4 Sky 812
5-7 Parchment 816

Florence

  36m

Attach yarn to hook with a slip knot, ch1, work all R1 sts into the 1-ch sp.

R1: ch3 (stch), 11tr, join with ss to 3rd ch of stch. {12 sts}

R2: ch3 (stch), tr in same st as ss, *ch2, skip 2 sts**, (2tr, ch2, 2tr) in next st*, rep from * to * 2x and * to ** 1x, 2tr in same st as first sts, ch1, join with dc to 3rd ch of stch. {4 sts, 1 2-ch sp on each side; 4 2-ch cnr sps}

R3: ch3 (stch), tr over joining dc, *skip 2 sts, 8tr in 2-ch sp, skip 2 sts**, (2tr, ch2, 2tr) in 2-ch sp*, rep from * to * 2x and * to ** 1x, 2tr in same sp as first sts, ch1, join with dc into 3rd ch of stch. {12 sts on each side; 4 2-ch cnr sps}

R4: ch3 (stch), tr over joining dc, *bptr around next 2 sts, htr in blo of next 8 sts, bptr around next 2 sts**, (2tr, ch2, 2tr) in 2-ch sp*, rep from * to * 2x and * to ** 1x, 2tr in same sp as first sts, ch1, join with dc into 3rd ch of stch. {16 sts on each side; 4 2-ch cnr sps}

R5: ch3 (stch), tr over joining dc, *ch4, skip 6 sts, dc in blo of next 4 sts, ch4, skip 6 sts**, (2tr, ch2, 2tr) in 2-ch sp*, rep from * to * 2x and * to ** 1x, 2tr in same sp as first sts, ch1, join with dc into 3rd ch of stch. {8 sts, 2 4-ch sps on each side; 4 2-ch cnr sps}

R6: ch3 (stch), tr over joining dc, *tr in next 2 sts, 4tr in 4-ch sp, tr in next 4 sts, 4tr in 4-ch sp, tr in next 2 sts**, (2tr, ch2, 2tr) in 2-ch sp*, rep from * to * 2x and * to ** 1x, 2tr in same sp as first sts, ch1, join with dc into 3rd ch of stch. {20 sts on each side; 4 2-ch cnr sps}

R7: dc over joining dc, *dc in next 20 sts**, (dc, ch2, dc) in 2-ch sp*, rep from * to * 2x and * to ** 1x, dc in same sp as first st, ch1, join with dc to first st. {22 sts on each side; 4 2-ch cnr sps}

R8: dc over joining dc, *dc in next 22 sts**, (dc, ch2, dc) in next st*, rep from * to * 2x and * to ** 1x, dc in same sp as first st, ch2, join with ss to first st. Fasten off. {24 sts on each side; 4 2-ch cnr sps}

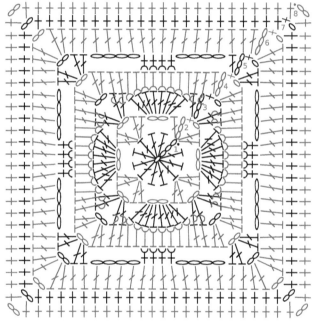

Bendigo Woollen Mills
Cotton 8 ply
1,3,5 and 7 Glacier 818
2,4,6 and 8 Grey Wisp 826

Cascade Ultra Pima
1-2 Turquoise 3733
3-4 Aqua 3732
5-6 Ice 3736
7-8 Natural 3718

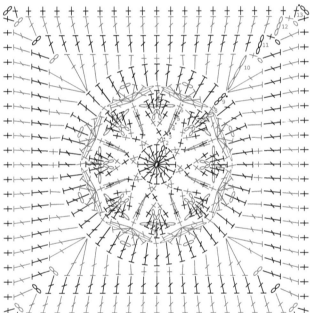

Anemone

  46m

TIP

- To make it easier, weave the end from the centre before starting R2.

NOTES

- R8: the ch1 at the start is not included in the st count.

Begin with a mc or ch4 and join the last ch to the first with a ss to make a loop.

R1: ch3 (stch), 15tr, join with ss to 3rd ch of stch. {16 sts}

R2: dc2tog over same st as ss and next st, *dc2tog over next 2 sts*, rep from * to * 6x, join with ss to first st. {8 sts}

R3: 2dc in same st as ss, 2dc in next 7 sts, join with ss to first st. {16 sts}

R4: dc in same st as ss, *(dc, ch4, dc) in next st**, dc in next st*, rep from * to * 6x and * to ** 1x, join with ss to first st. {24 sts, 8 4-ch sps}

R5: dc in same st as ss, dc in next st, *5tr in 4-ch sp**, dc in nexl 3 sts*, rep from * to * 6x and * to ** 1x, dc in next st, join with ss to first st. {64 sts}

R6: spike dc into R3 st below, *ch4, skip 7 sts, spike dc into R3 st below*, rep from * to * 6x, ch1, join with tr to first st. {8 sts, 8 4-ch sps}

R7: dc over joining tr, *(3tr, ch2, 3tr) in next st**, dc in 4-ch sp*, rep from * to * 6x and * to ** 1x, join with ss to first st. {56 sts, 8 2-ch sps}

R8: ch1, bpdc around st ss'd into, *ch3, skip (3 sts, 2-ch sp and 3 sts)**, bpdc around next st*, rep from * to * 6x and * to ** 1x, join with ss to first st. {8 sts, 8 3-ch sps}

R9: ch3 (stch), *5tr in 3-ch sp**, tr in next st*, rep from * to * 6x and * to ** 1x, join with ss to 3rd ch of stch. {48 sts}

R10: ch3 (stch), tr in same st as ss, *tr in next 2 sts, htr in next 2 sts, dc in next 3 sts, htr in next 2 sts, tr in next 2 sts**, (2tr, ch2, 2tr) in next st*, rep from * to * 2x and * to ** 1x, 2tr in same sp as first sts, ch1, join with dc to 3rd ch of stch. {15 sts on each side; 4 2-ch cnr sps}

R11: ch3 (stch), *tr in next 15 sts**, (tr, ch2, tr) in 2-ch sp*, rep from * to * 2x and * to ** 1x, tr in same sp as first st, ch1, join with dc to 3rd ch of stch. {17 sts on each side; 4 2-ch sp cnrs}

R12: ch3 (stch), *tr in next 17 sts**, (tr, ch2, tr) in 2-ch sp*, rep from * to * 2x and * to ** 1x, tr in same sp as first st, ch1, join with dc to 3rd ch of stch. {19 sts on each side; 4 2-ch sp cnrs}

R13: dc over joining dc, *dc in next 19 sts**, (dc, ch2, dc) in 2-ch sp*, rep from * to * 2x and * to ** 1x, dc in same sp as first st, ch2, join with ss to first st. Fasten off. {21 sts on each side; 4 2-ch cnr sps}

Paintbox Cotton DK
1 Banana Cream 421
2-3 Daffodil Yellow 422
4-5 Buttercup Yellow 423
6-7 Grass Green 430
8-13 Washed Teal 433

Bendigo Woollen Mills
Cotton 8 ply
1-2 Daffodil 806
3-5 Pomegranate 819
6-8 Kiwi 809
9-11 and 13 Snow 801
12 Pomegranate 819

Cascade Ultra Pima
1-4 Turquoise 3733
5-6 Aqua 3732
7-9 Ice 3736
10-13 Natural 3718

Framed

  🧶⟋46m

Begin with a mc or ch6 and join the last ch to the first with a ss to make a loop.

R1: ch3 (stch), * ch2, 3trcl, ch2**, tr*, rep from * to * 2x and * to ** 1x, join with ss to 3rd ch of stch. {8 sts, 8 2-ch sps}

R2: ch3 (stch), 3tr in same st as ss, *skip 2-ch sp, fpdc around next st, skip 2-ch sp**, 7tr in next st*, rep from * to * 2x and * to ** 1x, 3tr in same st as first sts, join with ss to 3rd ch of stch. {32 sts}

R3: dc in same st as ss, *bpdc around next 3 sts, ch3, skip 1 st, bpdc around next 3 sts**, (dc, ch3, dc) in next st*, rep from * to * 2x and * to ** 1x, dc in same st as first st, ch1, join with htr to first st.
{8 sts, 1 3-ch sp on each side; 4 3-ch cnr sps}

R4: ch3 (stch), 3tr over joining htr, *skip 1 st, dc2tog over next 2 sts, skip 1 st**, 7tr in 3-ch sp*, rep from * to * 6x and * to ** 1x, 3tr in same sp as first sts, join with ss to 3rd ch of stch. {64 sts}

R5: dc in same st as ss, *bpdc around next 3 sts, 3trcl in next st, bpdc around next 7 sts, 3trcl in next st, bpdc around next 3 sts**, (dc, ch2, dc) in next st*, rep from * to * 2x and * to ** 1x, dc in same st as first st, ch1, join with dc to first st. {17 sts on each side; 4 2-ch cnr sps}

R6: ch3 (stch), *tr in next 4 sts, fptr around next st, htr in next 2 sts, dc in next 3 sts, htr in next 2 sts, fptr around next st, tr in next 4 sts**, (tr, ch2, tr) in 2-ch sp*, rep from * to * 2x and * to ** 1x, tr in same sp as first st, ch1, join with dc to 3rd ch of stch. {19 sts on each side; 4 2-ch cnr sps}

R7: ch3 (stch), *fptr around next 19 sts**, (tr, ch2, tr) in 2-ch sp*, rep from * to * 2x and * to ** 1x, tr in same sp as first st, ch1, join with dc to 3rd ch of stch.
{21 sts on each side; 4 2-ch cnr sps}

R8: dc over joining dc, *skip R7 sts, tr in next 19 sts of R6 behind R7 sts**, (dc, ch2, dc) in 2-ch sp*, rep from * to * 2x and * to ** 1x, dc in same sp as first st, ch1, join with dc to first st. {21 sts on each side; 4 2-ch cnr sps}

R9: dc over joining dc, *dc in next 21 sts**, (dc, ch2, dc) in 2-ch sp*, rep from * to * 2x and * to ** 1x, dc in same sp as first st, ch2, join with ss to first st. Fasten off.
{23 sts on each side; 4 2-ch cnr sps}

Cascade Ultra Pima
1-2 Turquoise 3733
3-4 Aqua 3732
5-7 Ice 3736
8-9 Natural 3718

Erica Knight Studio Linen
1, 4-5, 7 and 9 Neo 404
2-3, 6 and 8 Milk 400

Granny Flower

  42m

Attach yarn to hook with a slip knot, ch1, work all R1 sts into the 1-ch sp.

R1: ch3 (stch), *ch2**, tr*, rep from * to * 6x and * to ** 1x, join with ss to 3rd ch of stch. {8 sts, 8 2-ch sps}

R2: dc in same st as ss, *(ss, ch3, 3tr, ch3, ss) in 2-ch sp**, dc in next st*, rep from * to * 6x and * to ** 1x, join with ss to first st. {48 sts, 16 3-ch sps}

R3: dc in same st as ss, *ch3, skip (ss, 3-ch sp, 3 sts, 3-ch sp and ss)**, dc in next st*, rep from * to * 6x and * to ** 1x, join with ss to first st. {8 sts, 8 3-ch sps}

R4: dc in same st as ss, *(ss, ch4, 3dtr, ch4, ss) in 3-ch sp**, dc in next st*, rep from * to * 6x and * to ** 1x, join with ss to first st. {48 sts, 16 4-ch sps}

R5: dc in same st as ss, *ch3, skip (ss, 4-ch sp, 3 sts, 4-ch sp and ss)**, dc in next st*, rep from * to * 6x and * to ** 1x, join with ss to first st. {8 sts, 8 3-ch sps}

R6: ch3 (stch), 2tr in same st as ss, *ch1, skip 3-ch sp, 3tr in next st, ch1, skip 3-ch sp**, (3tr, ch2, 3tr) in next st*, rep from * to * 2x and * to ** 1x, 3tr in same st as first sts, ch1, join with dc to 3rd ch of stch.
{9 sts, 2 1-ch sps on each side; 4 2-ch cnr sps}

R7: ch3 (stch), 2tr over joining dc, *2x [ch1, skip 3 sts, 3tr in 1-ch sp], ch1, skip 3tr**, (3tr, ch2, 3tr) in 2-ch sp*, rep from * to * 2x and * to ** 1x, 3tr in same sp as first sts, ch1, join with dc into 3rd ch of stch.
{12 sts, 3 1-ch sps on each side; 4 2-ch cnr sps}

R8: ch3 (stch), 2tr over joining dc, *3x [ch1, skip 3 sts, 3tr in 1-ch sp], ch1, skip 3tr**, (3tr, ch2, 3tr) in 2-ch sp*, rep from * to * 2x and * to ** 1x, 3tr in same sp as first sts, ch1, join with dc into 3rd ch of stch.
{15 sts, 4 1-ch sps on each side; 4 2-ch cnr sps}

R9: ch3 (stch), 2tr over joining dc, *4x [ch1, skip 3 sts, 3tr in 1-ch sp], ch1, skip 3tr**, (3tr, ch2, 3tr) in 2-ch sp*, rep from * to * 2x and * to ** 1x, 3tr in same sp as first sts, ch1, join with dc to 3rd ch of stch.
{18 sts, 5 1-ch sps on each side; 4 2-ch cnr sps}

R10: dc over joining dc, *5x [dc in next 3 sts, dc in 1-ch sp], dc in next 3 sts**, (dc, ch2, dc) in 2-ch sp*, rep from * to * 2x and * to ** 1x, dc in same sp as first st, ch2, join with ss to first st. Fasten off. {25 sts on each side; 4 2-ch cnr sps}

Susan's Granny Flower
Scheepjes Catona
1 Saffron 249
2-4 Scarlet 192
5-8 Silver Blue 528
9-10 Deep Ocean Green 391
www.instagram.com/suregal27

Cascade Ultra Pima
1 Turquoise 3733
2-3 Aqua 3732
4-5 Ice 3736
6-10 Natural 3718

D'Urville

 ＠🧶 41m ✂

NOTES

- R1: the ch1 at the start is not included in the st count.

Special Stitch: modified treble (mtr)- a normal tr with an extra step to anchor the top sts to the square.

Begin your tr as normal, yo, insert hook in ch sp, pull a loop to the front, yo, pull through 2 loops on hook, insert your hook in the st behind from the previous round and pull a loop to the front and through both loops on the hook.

Attach yarn to hook with a slip knot, ch1, work all R1 sts into the 1-ch sp.

R1: ch1, 12dc, join with ss to first st. {12 sts}

R2: ch3 (stch), 2tr in same st as ss, *tr2tog in blo of next 2 sts**, 5tr in next st*, rep from * to * 2x and * to ** 1x, 2tr in same sp as first sts, join with ss to 3rd ch of stch. {24 sts}

R3: dc in same st as ss, *ch2, skip 2 sts of R2, tr in flo of next 2 sts of R1, ch2, skip 3 sts of R2**, dc in next st*, rep from * to * 2x and * to ** 1x, join with ss to first st. {2 sts, 2 2-ch sps on each side; 4 1-st cnrs}

R4: ch3 (stch), 2tr in same st as ss, *skip (R3 sts and ch sps), tr in next 5 sts of R2**, 5tr in next st of R3*, rep from * to * 2x and * to **, 2tr in same sp as first sts, join with ss to 3rd ch of stch. {5 sts on each side; 4 5-st cnrs}

R5: dc in same st as ss, *ch2, skip 2 sts of R4, 2tr in 2-ch sp of R3, ch2, skip 2 sts of R3, 2tr in 2-ch sp of R3, ch2, skip 2 sts of R4**, dc in next st of R4*, rep from * to * 2x and * to ** 1x, join with ss to first st. {4 sts, 3 2-ch sps on each side; 4 1-st cnrs}

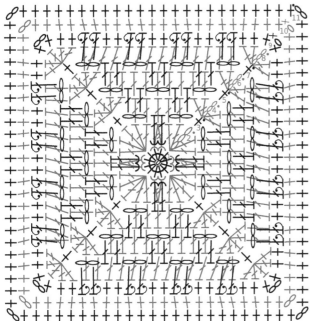

R6: ch3 (stch), 2tr in same st as ss, *skip (R5 sts and ch sps), tr in next 9 sts of R4**, 5tr in next st of R5*, rep from * to * 2x and * to **, 2tr in same sp as first sts, join with ss to 3rd ch of stch. {9 sts on each side; 4 5-st cnrs}

R7: dc in same st as ss, *ch2, skip 2 sts of R6, 2x [2tr in 2-ch sp of R5, ch2, skip 2 sts of R5], 2tr in 2-ch sp of R5, ch2, skip 2 sts of R6**, dc in next st of R6*, rep from * to * 2x and * to ** 1x, join with ss to first st. {6 sts, 4 2-ch sps on each side; 4 1-st cnrs}

R8: ch3 (stch), 2tr in same st as ss, *skip (R7 sts and ch sps), tr in next 12 sts of R6, 2tr in next st**, 5tr in next st of R7*, rep from * to * 2x and * to **, 2tr in same sp as first sts, join with ss to 3rd ch of stch. {14 sts on each side; 4 5-st cnrs}

R9: dc in same st as ss, *dc in next 2 sts of R8, 4x [2mtr in 2-ch sps of R7 and next sts of R8, dc in next 2 sts of R8]**, (dc, ch2, dc) in next st of R8*, rep from * to * 2x and * to ** 1x, dc in same sp as first st, ch1, join with dc to first st. {20 sts on each side; 4 2-ch cnr sps}

R10: dc over joining dc, *dc in next 20 sts**, (dc, ch2, dc) in 2-ch sp*, rep from * to * 2x and * to ** 1x, dc in same sp as first st, ch1, join with dc to first st. {22 sts on each side; 4 2-ch cnr sps}

R11: dc over joining dc, *dc in next 22 sts**, (dc, ch2, dc) in next st*, rep from * to * 2x and * to ** 1x, dc in same sp as first st, ch2, join with ss to first st. Fasten off. {24 sts on each side; 4 2-ch cnr sps}

To extend

Stop at the end of R7, rep R6 and R7 as many times as needed, increasing the numbers as follows:

R6 "...tr in next #+4 sts of R#+2" {#+4 sts ...}

R7 "... all R#+2, #+1x [..." {#+2 sts, #+1 2-ch sps ...}

Then add R8 "...tr in next # sts, working 2 sts in the last st of the round 2 rounds prior..."

Then add R9, working as many [mtr repeats] as required, then add the remaining rounds working a st in each st of the previous round.

Killarney

 34m

TIP
- Pull up a long loop when making the fp sts to avoid creating a dip along the edge.

Attach yarn to hook with a slip knot, ch1, work all R1 sts into the 1-ch sp.

R1: ch3 (stch), 2tr, *ch2, 3tr*, rep from * to * 2x, ch1, join with dc to 3rd ch of stch.
{3 sts on each side; 4 2-ch cnr sps}

R2: ch3 (stch), tr over joining dc, *skip 1 st, fptr around next st, skip 1 st**, (2tr, ch2, 2tr) in 2-ch sp*, rep from * to * 2x and * to ** 1x, 2tr in same sp as first sts, ch1, join with dc to 3rd ch of stch. {5 sts on each side; 4 2-ch cnr sps}

R3: ch3 (stch), tr over joining dc, *tr in next st, fptr around next 3 sts, tr in next st**, (2tr, ch2, 2tr) in 2-ch sp*, rep from * to * 2x and * to ** 1x, 2tr in same sp as first sts, ch1, join with dc to 3rd ch of stch.
{9 sts on each side; 4 2-ch cnr sps}

R4: ch3 (stch), tr over joining dc, *tr in next 3 sts, fptr around next 3 sts, tr in next 3 sts**, (2tr, ch2, 2tr) in 2-ch sp*, rep from * to * 2x and * to ** 1x, 2tr in same sp as first sts, ch1, join with dc to 3rd ch of stch.
{13 sts on each side; 4 2-ch cnr sps}

R5: ch3 (stch), tr over joining dc, *tr in next 5 sts, fptr around next 3 sts, tr in next 5 sts**, (2tr, ch2, 2tr) in 2-ch sp*, rep from * to * 2x and * to ** 1x, 2tr in same sp as first sts, ch1, join with dc to 3rd ch of stch.
{17 sts on each side; 4 2-ch cnr sps}

R6: ch3 (stch), tr over joining dc, *tr in next 7 sts, fptr around next 3 sts, tr in next 7 sts**, (2tr, ch2, 2tr) in 2-ch sp*, rep from * to * 2x and * to ** 1x, 2tr in same sp as first sts, ch1, join with dc to 3rd ch of stch.
{21 sts on each side; 4 2-ch cnr sps}

R7: dc over joining dc, *dc in next 21 sts**, (dc, ch2, dc) in 2-ch sp*, rep from * to * 2x and * to ** 1x, dc in same sp as first st, ch2, join with ss to first st. Fasten off.
{23 sts on each side; 4 2-ch cnr sps}

To extend

Stop at the end of R6, rep R6 as many times as needed, increasing the numbers as follows:

R6 "tr in next #+2 ... tr in next #+2 sts" {#+4 sts ...}

Then add R7 working a st in each st on the side.

Cascade Ultra Pima
1-2 Turquoise 3733
3-4 Aqua 3732
5-6 Ice 3736
7 Natural 3718

Great Ocean Road Woollen Mill
100% Alpaca
1-3 Champagne
4-5 Toffee
6-7 Dark Brown

Ollie

 33m

NOTES

• R5: the ch1 at the start is not included in the st count.

Attach yarn to hook with a slip knot, ch1, work all R1 sts into the 1-ch sp.

R1: ch3 (stch), *ch1, tr*, rep from * to * 6x, join with dc to 3rd ch of stch. {8 sts, 8 1-ch sps}

R2: dc over joining dc, *dc in next st**, (dc, ch2, dc) in 1-ch sp*, rep from * to * 6x and * to ** 1x, dc in same sp as first st, ch2, join with ss to first st.
{3 sts on each side; 8 2-ch sps}

R3: ch3 (stch), tr in next 2 sts, *ch2, skip 2-ch sp, tr in next 3 sts*, rep from * to * 6x, ch1, join with dc to 3rd ch of stch. {3 sts on each side, 8 2-ch sps}

R4: dc over joining dc, *dc in next 3 sts**, (dc, ch2, dc) in 2-ch sp*, rep from * to * 6x and * to ** 1x, dc in same sp as first st, ch1, join with dc to first st.
{5 sts on each side; 8 2-ch sps}

R5: ch1, htr over joining dc, *htr in next 5 sts**, (htr, ch1, htr) in 2-ch sp*, rep from * to * 6x and * to ** 1x, htr in same sp as first st, ch1, join with ss to first st.
{7 sts on each side; 8 1-ch sps}

R6: htr in lbv of same st as ss, *tr in lbv of next 5 sts, htr in lbv of next st**, ch1, skip 1-ch sp, htr in lbv of next st*, rep from * to * 6x and from * to ** 1x, join with dc to first st.
{7 sts on each side, 8 1-ch sps}

R7: ch4 (stch), *ch1, skip 1 st, tr in next st, 2x [ch1, skip 1 st, htr ln next st], ch1, skip 1 st, dc in 1-ch sp, 2x [ch1, skip 1 st, htr in next st], ch1, skip 1 st, tr in next st, ch1, skip 1 st**, (dtr, ch2, dtr) in 1-ch sp*, rep from * to * 2x and * to ** 1x, dtr in same sp as first st, ch1, join with dc to 4th ch of stch.
{9 sts, 8 1-ch sps on each side; 4 2-ch cnr sps}

R8: ch3 (stch), *8x [tr in next st, tr in 1-ch sp], tr in next st**, (tr, ch2, tr) in 2-ch sp*, rep from * to * 2x and * to ** 1x, tr in same sp as first st, ch1, join with dc to 3rd ch of stch.
{19 sts on each side; 4 2-ch cnr sps}

R9: dc over joining dc, *dc in next 19 sts**, (dc, ch2, dc) in 2-ch sp*, rep from * to * 2x and * to ** 1x, dc in same sp as first st, ch2, join with ss to first st. Fasten off.
{21 sts on each side; 4 2-ch cnr sps}

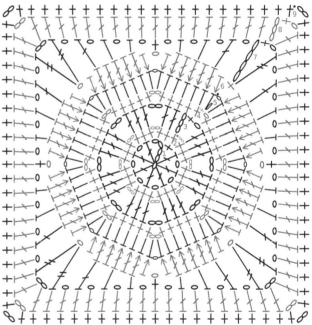

Bendigo Woollen Mills
Cotton 8 ply
1-5 Glacier 818
6 Grey Wisp 826
7-9 Storm Cloud 827

Cascade Ultra Pima
1-3 Turquoise 3733
4-5 Aqua 3732
6-7 Ice 3736
8-9 Natural 3718

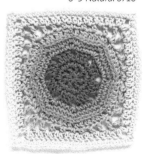

Iron Lace

  44m

NOTES

- **R9:** the ch3 (stch) and 4trpc count as 1 5trpc.

Begin with a mc or ch4 and join the last ch to the first with a ss to make a loop.

R1: ch3 (stch), 15tr, join with ss to 3rd ch of stch. {16 sts}

R2: 8x (dc2tog over next 2 sts), join with ss to first st. {8 sts}

R3: 2dc in same st as ss, 2dc in next 7 sts, join with ss to first st. {16 sts}

R4: ch3 (stch), *pc in next st, 3tr in next st, pc in next st**, (tr, ch2, tr) in next st*, rep from * to * 2x and * to ** 1x, tr in same st as first st, ch1, join with dc to 3rd ch of stch. {7 sts on each side; 4 2-ch cnr sps}

R5: ch3 (stch), tr over joining dc, *tr in next st, fptr around next st, tr in next 3 sts, fptr around next st, tr in next st**, 3tr in 2-ch sp*, rep from * to * 2x and * to ** 1x, tr in same sp as first sts, join with ss to 3rd ch of stch. {7 sts on each side; 4 3-st cnrs}

R6: ch3 (stch), tr in same st as ss, *tr2tog over next 2 sts, ch2, fptr around next st, tr in next 3 sts, fptr around next st, ch2, tr2tog over next 2 sts**, 3tr in next st*, rep from * to * 2x and * to ** 1x, tr in same st as first sts, join with ss to 3rd ch of stch. {7 sts, 2 2-ch sps on each side; 4 3-st cnrs}

R7: ch3 (stch), tr in same st as ss, *tr2tog over next 2 sts, ch3, skip 2-ch sp, fptr around next st, tr in next st, ch2, fpdc around next st, ch2, tr in next st, fptr around next st, ch3, skip 2-ch sp, tr2tog over next 2 sts**, 3tr in next st*, rep from * to * 2x and * to ** 1x, tr in same st as first sts, join with ss to 3rd ch of stch. {7 sts, 2 2-ch sps, 2 3-ch sps on each side; 4 3-st cnrs}

R8: ch3 (stch), *tr2tog over next 2 sts, ch5, skip 3-ch sp, fptr around next st, 3trpc in next st, ch2, skip (2-ch sp, 1 st and 2-ch sp), 3trpc in next st, fptr around next st, ch5, skip 3-ch sp, tr2tog over next 2 sts**, (tr, ch1, tr) in next st*, rep from * to * 2x and * to ** 1x, tr in same sp as first st, join with dc to 3rd ch of stch.
{8 sts, 2 5-ch sps, 1 2-ch sp on each side; 4 1-ch cnr sps}

R9: ch3 (stch), 4trpc over joining dc, *ch2, dc in next 2 sts, 4dc in 5-ch sp, dc in next st, fpdc around next st, 2dc in 2-ch sp, fpdc around next st, dc in next st, 4dc in 5-ch sp, dc in next 2 sts, ch2**, pc in 1-ch sp*, rep from * to * 2x and * to ** 1x, join with ss to first sts.
{18 sts, 2 2-ch sps on each side; 4 1-st cnrs}

R10: dc in same st as ss, *dc in 2-ch sp, dc in next 18 sts, dc in 2-ch sp**, (dc, ch2, dc) in next st*, rep from * to * 2x and * to ** 1x, dc in same st as first st, ch1, join with dc to first st. {22 sts on each side; 4 2-ch cnr sps}

R11: dc over joining dc, *dc in next 22 sts**, (dc, ch2, dc) in 2-ch sp*, rep from * to * 2x and * to ** 1x, dc in same sp as first st, ch2, join with ss to first st. Fasten off.
{24 sts on each side; 4 2-ch cnr sps}

Emily's Iron Lace 1
Stylecraft Special DK
1 Lemon
2-4 Sunshine
5 Apricot
6 Candyfloss
7 Fondant
8 Clematis
9 Cloud Blue
10 Sherbet
11 Spring Green
Extra round Aspen
www.theloopystitch.com

Emily's Iron Lace 2
Stylecraft Special DK
1-3 and 9 Boysenberry
4 and 10 Plum
5 Duck Egg
6 Sage
7 Petrol
8 and 11 Parchment
www.theloopystitch.com

Cascade Ultra Pima
1-4 Turquoise 3733
5-8 Aqua 3732
9 Ice 3736
10-11 Natural 3718

Solomon

 31m

Begin with a mc or ch4 and join the last ch to the first with a ss to make a loop.

R1: ch3 (stch), 15tr, join with ss to 3rd ch of stch. {16 sts}

R2: dc in same st as ss, *ch2, dc in next st*, rep from * to * 14x, ch2, join with ss to first st. {16 sts, 16 2-ch sps}

R3: *(dc, htr, tr, ch2, tr, htr, dc) in 2-ch sp**, ch1, skip (1 st, 2-ch sp and 1 st)*, rep from * to * 6x and * to ** 1x, join with dc to first st. {48 sts, 8 1-ch sps, 8 2-ch sps}

R4: ss over joining dc and 2-ch sp of R2, ch3 (stch), *ch2, skip 3 sts, dc in 2-ch sp, ch2, skip 3 sts**, hdtr over 1-ch sp of R3 and 2-ch sp of R2*, rep from * to * 6x and * to ** 1x, join with ss to 3rd ch of stch. {16 sts, 16 2-ch sps}

R5: dc in same st as ss, *2dc in 2-ch sp**, dc in next st*, rep from * to * 14x and * to ** 1x, join with ss to first st. {48 sts}

R6: ch3 (stch), *ch2, skip 1 st**, tr in next st*, rep from * to * 22x and * to ** 1x, join with ss to 3rd ch of stch. {24 sts, 24 2-ch sps}

R7: ch3 (stch), *skip 2-ch sp, 4x [dc in next st, 2dc in 2-ch sp], dc in next st, skip 2-ch sp**, (tr, ch4, tr) in next st*, rep from * to * 2x and * to ** 1x, tr in same sp as first st, ch1, join with tr to 3rd ch of stch. {15 sts on each side; 4 4-ch cnr sps}

R8: 2dc over joining tr, *dc in next 15 sts**, (2dc, ch2, 2dc) in 4-ch sp*, rep from * to * 2x and * to ** 1x, 2dc in same sp as first sts, ch1, join with dc to first st. {19 sts on each side; 4 2-ch cnr sps}

R9: dc over joining dc, *9x [ch1, skip 1 st, dc in next st], ch1, skip 1 st**, (dc, ch2, dc) in 2-ch sp*, rep from * to * 2x and * to ** 1x, dc in same sp as first st, ch1, join with dc to first st. {11 sts, 10 1-ch sps on each side; 4 2-ch cnr sps}

R10: dc over joining dc, *10x [dc in next st, dc in 1-ch sp], dc in next st**, (dc, ch2, dc) in 2-ch sp*, rep from * to * 2x and * to ** 1x, dc in same sp as first st, ch2, join with ss to first st. Fasten off. {23 sts on each side; 4 2-ch cnr sps}

Cascade Ultra Pima
1-2 Turquoise 3733
3 Aqua 3732
4-6 Ice 3736
7-10 Natural 3718

Paintbox Cotton DK
1-2 and 4-6 Lipstick Pink 452
3 Raspberry Pink 444
7-10 Kingfisher Blue 435

Kruis

   39m

Attach yarn to hook with a slip knot, ch1, work all R1 sts into the 1-ch sp.

R1: ch3 (stch), 11tr, join with ss to 3rd ch of stch. {12 sts}

R2: ch3 (stch), 2tr in same sp as ss, *fptr around next st, ch1, fptr around next st**, (3tr, ch2, 3tr) in next st*, rep from * to * 2x and * to ** 1x, 3tr in same sp as first sts, ch1, join with dc to 3rd ch of stch. {8 sts, 1 1-ch sp on each side; 4 2-ch cnr sps}

R3: ch3 (stch), *tr in next st, tr2tog over next 2 sts, fptr around next st, ch1, skip 1-ch sp, fptr around next st, tr2tog over next 2 sts, tr in next st**, (tr, ch2, tr) in 2-ch sp*, rep from * to * 2x and * to ** 1x, tr in same sp as first st, ch1, join with dc to 3rd ch of stch. {8 sts, 1 1-ch sp on each side; 4 2-ch cnr sps}

R4: ch3 (stch), *tr in next st, tr2tog over next 2 sts, fptr around next st, ch2, skip 1-ch sp, fptr around next st, tr2tog over next 2 sts, tr in next st**, (tr, ch2, tr) in 2-ch sp*, rep from * to * 2x and * to ** 1x, tr in same sp as first st, ch1, join with dc to 3rd ch of stch. {8 sts, 1 2-ch sp on each side; 4 2-ch cnr sps}

R5: dc over joining dc, *dc in next 3 sts, fptr around next st, (tr, ch2, tr) in 2-ch sp, fptr around next st, dc in next 3 sts**, (dc, ch2, dc) in 2-ch sp*, rep from * to * 2x and * to ** 1x, dc in same sp as first st, ch1, join with dc to first st. {12 sts, 1 2-ch sp on each side; 4 2-ch cnr sps}

R6: dc over joining dc, *dc in next 4 sts, fptr around next st, tr in next st, (tr, ch2, tr) in 2-ch sp, tr in next st, fptr around next st, dc in next 4 sts**, (dc, ch2, dc) in 2-ch sp*, rep from * to * 2x and * to ** 1x, dc in same sp as first st, ch1, join with dc to first st. {16 sts, 1 2-ch sp on each side; 4 2-ch cnr sps}

R7: ch3 (stch), tr over joining dc, *tr in next 4 sts, tr2tog over next 2 sts, fptr around last st worked into, skip 1 st, dc in next st, dc in 2-ch sp, dc in next st, skip 1 st, fptr around next st, tr2tog beginning with st just worked around and in next st, tr in next 4 sts**, (2tr, ch2, 2tr) in 2-ch sp*, rep from * to * 2x and * to ** 1x, 2tr in same sp as first sts, ch1, join with dc to 3rd ch of stch. {19 sts on each side; 4 2-ch cnr sps}

R8: dc over joining dc, *dc in next 8 sts, fphtr around st just worked into, skip 1 st, dc in next st, skip 1 st, fphtr around next st, dc in st just worked around, dc in next 7 sts**, (dc, ch2, dc) in 2-ch sp*, rep from * to * 2x and * to ** 1x, dc in same sp as first st, ch1, join with dc to first st. {21 sts on each side; 4 2-ch cnr sps}

R9: dc over joining dc, *dc in next 10 sts, fptr2tog over the next 2 fp sts skipping st between them, dc in st just worked around, dc in next 9 sts**, (dc, ch2, dc) in 2-ch sp*, rep from * to * 2x and * to ** 1x, dc in same sp as first st, ch2, join with ss to first st. Fasten off. {23 sts on each side; 4 2-ch cnr sps}

Cascade Ultra Pima
1-3 Turquoise 3733
4-6 Aqua 3732
7-8 Ice 3736
9 Natural 3718

Bendigo Woollen Mills
Cotton 8 ply
1-9 French Navy 814

Bulaklak

  48m

NOTES

- R1, R5 and R7: the ch st/s at the start do not count towards st counts.

Attach yarn to hook with a slip knot, ch1, work all R1 sts into the 1-ch sp.

R1: ch1, 8dc, join with ss to first st. {8 sts}

R2: ch3 (stch), tr in same st as ss, 2tr in next 7 sts, join with ss to 3rd ch of stch. {16 sts}

R3: dc in same st as ss, *ch3, skip 1 st, dc in next st*, rep from * to * 6x, ch3, join with ss to first st. {8 sts, 8 3-ch loops}

R4: dc in same st as ss, *(2tr, ch1, 2tr) in 3-ch sp**, dc in next st*, rep from * to * 6x and * to ** 1x, join with ss to first st. {40 sts; 8 1-ch sps}

R5: ch1, bpdc around st below of R3, *ch7, skip (2 sts, 1-ch sp and 2 sts)**, bpdc around st below of R3*, rep from * to * 6x and * to ** 1x, join with ss to first st. {8 sts, 8 7-ch sps}

R6: dc in same st as ss, *(2tr, 2hdtr, 2dtr, ch2, 2dtr, 2hdtr, 2tr) in 7-ch sp**, dc in next st*, rep from * to * 6x and * to ** 1x, join with ss to first st. {104 sts, 8 2-ch sps}

R7: ch2, bpdc around st below of R3, *ch4, skip (6 sts, 2-ch sp and 6 sts)**, bpdc around st below of R3*, rep from * to * 6x and * to ** 1x, join with ss to first st. {8 sts, 8 4-ch sps}

R8: ch3 (stch), *4hdtr in 4-ch sp**, hdtr in next st*, rep from * to * 6x and * to ** 1x, join with ss to 3rd ch of stch. {40 sts}

R9: ch4 (stch), hdtr in same st as ss, *tr in next 2 sts, htr in next 2 sts, dc in next st, htr in next 2 sts, tr in next 2 sts**, (hdtr, dtr, ch2, dtr, hdtr) in next st*, rep from * to * 2x and * to ** 1x, (hdtr, dtr) in same sp as first sts, ch1, join with dc to 4th ch of stch. {13 sts on each side; 4 2-ch cnr sps}

R10: ch3 (stch), 4hdtr over joining dc, *skip 3 sts, dc in next 2 sts, skip 1 st, (3tr, ch1, 3tr) in next st, skip 1 st, dc in next 2 sts, skip 3 sts**, (5hdtr, ch2, 5hdtr) in 2-ch sp*, rep from * to * 2x and * to ** 1x, 5hdtr in same sp as first sts, ch1, join with dc to 3rd ch of stch.
{20 sts, 1 1-ch sp on each side; 4 2-ch cnr sps}

R11: dc over joining dc, *dc in next 3 sts, ch2, skip 3 sts, tr in next st, ch2, skip 3 sts, dc in 1-ch sp, ch2, skip 3 sts, tr in next st, ch2, skip 3 sts, dc in next 3 sts**, (dc, ch2, dc) in 2-ch sp*, rep from * to * 2x and * to ** 1x, dc in same sp as first st, ch1, join with dc to first st.
{11 sts, 4 2-ch sps on each side; 4 2-ch cnr sps}

R12: dc over joining dc, *dc in next 4 sts, 3x [2dc in 2-ch sp, dc in next st], 2dc in 2-ch sp, dc in next 4 sts**, (dc, ch2, dc) in 2-ch sp*, rep from * to * 2x and * to ** 1x, dc in same sp as first st, ch2, join with ss to first st. Fasten off.
{21 sts on each side; 4 2-ch cnr sps}

Bendigo Woollen Mills
Cotton 4 ply
1-2 Daffodil 806
3-7 Pomegranate 819
8-10 Kiwi 809
11-12 Parchment 816

Alia's Bulaklak
Scheepjes Catona
1-3 Lemon 280
4 Tulip 222
5-7 Shocking Pink 114
8-10 Apple Green 513
11-12 Tropic 253
www.thelittlebee.co.nz

Cascade Ultra Pima
1-3 Turquoise 3733
4-7 Aqua 3732
8-10 Ice 3736
11-12 Natural 3718

Quion

  34m

Attach yarn to hook with a slip knot, ch1, work all R1 sts into the 1-ch sp.

R1: ch3 (stch), 2tr, *ch4, 3tr*, rep from * to * 1x, ch1, join with tr to 3rd ch of stch.
{3 sts on each side; 3 4-ch cnr sps}

R2: ch3 (stch), 2tr over joining tr, *tr in next 3 sts**, (3tr, ch2, 3tr) in 4-ch sp*, rep from * to * 1x and * to ** 1x, 3tr in same sp as first sts, ch1, join with dc to 3rd ch of stch.
{9 sts on each side; 3 2-ch cnr sps}

R3: ch3 (stch), tr over joining dc, * tr in next 9 sts**, (2tr, ch2, 2tr) in 2-ch sp*, rep from * to * 1x and * to ** 1x, 2tr in same sp as first sts, ch1, join with dc to 3rd ch of stch.
{13 sts on each side; 3 2-ch cnr sps}

R4: ch3 (stch), tr over joining dc, *htr in lbv of next 2 sts, tr in lbv of next 2 sts, hdtr in lbv of next 2 sts, dtr in lbv of next st, hdtr in lbv of next 2 sts, tr in lbv of next 2 sts, htr in lbv of next 2 sts**, 3tr in 2-ch sp*, rep from * to * 1x and * to ** 1x, tr in same sp as first sts, join with ss to 3rd ch of stch.
{48 sts}

R5: dc in same st as ss, dc in next 47 sts, join with ss to first st. {48 sts}

R6: ch2 (stch), *skip 1 st**, (htr, ch1, htr) in next st*, rep from * to * 22x and * to ** 1x, htr in same st as ss, join with dc to 2nd ch of stch. {48 sts, 24 1-ch-sps}

R7: dc over joining dc, *skip 1 st, dc in next st**, 2dc in 1-ch sp*, rep from * to * 22x and * to ** 1x, dc in same sp as first st, join with ss to first st. {72 sts}

R8: ch4 (stch), 3dtr in same st as ss, *skip 2 sts, dc in next 13 sts, skip 2 sts**, 7dtr in next st*, rep from * to * 2x and * to ** 1x, 3dtr in same st as first sts, join with ss to 4th ch of stch. {13 sts on each side; 4 7-st cnrs}

R9: dc in same st as ss, *dc in next 3 sts, htr in next st, dc in next 11 sts, htr in next st, dc in next 3 sts**, (dc, ch2, dc) in next st*, rep from * to * 2x and * to ** 1x, dc in same st as first st, ch2, join with ss to first st. Fasten off.
{21 sts on each side; 4 2-ch cnr sps}

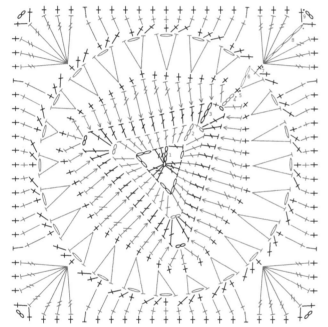

Cascade Ultra Pima
1-3 Turquoise 3733
4-5 Aqua 3732
6-7 Ice 3736
8-9 Natural 3718

Marianne's Quion
1 Yellow Katia Capri 82118
2 and 8 Bright Pink Durable Coral 236
3 Light Pink Durable Coral 203
4-6 Off-White Durable Coral 326
7 Bright Green Katia Capri 82105
9 Bright Blue Katia Capri 82101
www.marrose-ccc.com

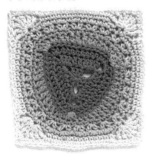 

Louloudia

   36m

Attach yarn to hook with a slip knot, ch1, work all R1 sts into the 1-ch sp.

R1: ch3 (stch), 11tr, join with ss to 3rd ch of stch. {12 sts}

R2: ch3 (stch), tr in same st as ss, *ch2, skip 1 st**, 2tr in next st*, rep from * to * 4x and * to ** 1x, join with ss to 3rd ch of stch. {12 sts, 6 2-ch sps}

R3: ch3 (stch), 3tr in same st as ss, picot, 4tr in next st, *skip 2-ch sp, 4tr in next st, picot, 4tr in next st*, rep from * to * 4x, join with ss to 3rd ch of stch. {54 sts}

R4: *spike dc into skipped st below of R1**, ch4*, rep from * to * 4x and * to ** 1x, ch1, join with htr to first st. {6 sts, 6 4-ch sps}

R5: dc over joining htr, *ch2, 3tr in next st, ch2**, dc in 4-ch sp*, rep from * to * 4x and * to ** 1x, join with ss to first st. {24 sts, 12 2-ch sps}

R6: dc in same st as ss, *skip 2-ch sp, (dc, htr) in next st, (2tr, ch1, 2tr) in next st, (htr, dc) in next st, skip 2-ch sp**, dc in next st*, rep from * to * 4x and * to ** 1x, join with ss to first st. {54 sts}

R7: ch3 (stch), *ch2, skip 2 sts, htr in lbv of next st, ch2, skip 1 st, dc in 1-ch sp, ch2, skip 1 st, htr in lbv of next st, ch2, skip 2 sts**, tr in next st*, rep from * to * 4x and * to ** 1x, join with ss to 3rd ch of stch. {24 sts, 24 2-ch sps}

R8: ch4 (stch), *ch1, hdtr in 2-ch sp, ch1, skip 1 st, tr in 2-ch sp, ch1, htr in next st, ch1, dc in 2-ch sp, ch1, skip 1 st, dc in 2-ch sp, ch1, htr in next st, ch1, tr in 2-ch sp, ch1, skip 1 st, hdtr in 2-ch sp, ch1**, (dtr, ch2, dtr) in next st*, rep from * to * 2x and * to ** 1x, dtr in same sp as first st, ch1, join with dc to 4th ch of stch. {10 sts, 9 1-ch sps on each side; 4 2-ch cnr sps}

R9: ch3 (stch), *9x [tr in next st, tr in 1-ch sp], tr in next st**, (tr, ch2, tr) in 2-ch sp*, rep from * to * 2x and * to ** 1x, tr in same sp as first st, ch1, join with dc to 3rd ch of stch. {21 sts on each side; 4 2-ch cnr sps}

R10: dc over joining dc, *dc in next 21 sts**, (dc, ch2, dc) in next st*, rep from * to * 2x and * to ** 1x, dc in same sp as first st, ch2, join with ss to first st. Fasten off. {23 sts on each side; 4 2-ch cnr sps}

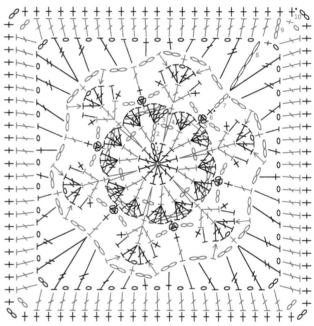

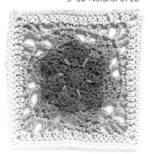

Narrawong

  33m

Attach yarn to hook with a slip knot, ch1, work all R1 sts into the 1-ch sp.

R1: ch3 (stch), *ch1, tr*, rep from * to * 10x, ch1, join with ss to 3rd ch of stch. {12 sts, 12 1-ch sps}

R2: ch3 (stch), fptr around st ss'd into, *ch1, skip 1-ch sp, tr in next st, fptr around same st*, rep from * to * 10x, ch1, skip 1-ch sp, join with ss to 3rd ch of stch. {24 sts, 12 1-ch sps}

R3: dc in same st as ss, dc in next st, dc in 1-ch sp, *dc in next 2 sts, dc in 1-ch sp*, rep from * to * 10x, join with ss to first st. {36 sts}

R4: ch3 (stch), *ch2, skip 1 st**, tr in next st*, rep from * to * 16x and * to ** 1x, join with ss to 3rd ch of stch. {18 sts, 18 2-ch sps}

R5: ch3 (stch), *2tr in 2-ch sp**, tr in next st*, rep from * to * 16x and * to ** 1x, join with ss to 3rd ch of stch. {54 sts}

R6: dc in same st as ss, dc in next st, 2dc in next st, *dc in next 2 sts, 2dc in next st*, rep from * to * 16x, join with ss to first st. {72 sts}

R7: ch3 (stch), 2tr in same st as ss, *skip 2 sts, dc in next 13 sts, skip 2 sts**, 5tr in next st*, rep from * to * 2x and * to ** 1x, 2tr in same sp as first sts, join with ss to 3rd ch of stch. {13 sts on each side; 4 5-st cnrs}

R8: ch3 (stch), tr in same st as ss, *tr in next 4 sts, dc in next 9 sts, tr in next 4 sts**, 3tr in next st*, rep from * to * 2x and * to ** 1x, tr in same sp as first sts, join with ss to 3rd ch of stch. {17 sts on each side; 4 3-st cnrs}

R9: 2dc in same st as ss, *dc in next 19 sts**, (2dc, ch2, 2dc) in next st*, rep from * to * 2x and * to ** 1x, 2dc in same sp as first sts, ch2, join with ss to first st. Fasten off. {23 sts on each side; 4 2-ch sp cnrs}

Cascade Ultra Pima
1-3 Turquoise 3733
4-6 Aqua 3732
7-8 Ice 3736
9 Natural 3718

*Bendigo Woollen Mills
Luxury 8 ply*
1-2 and 7-8 Leaf 358
3-6 and 9 Blue Denim 363

Spike

 38m

Attach yarn to hook with a slip knot, ch1, work all R1 sts into the 1-ch sp.

R1: ch3 (stch), 11tr, join with ss to 3rd ch of stch. {12 sts}

R2: ch3 (stch), 2tr in same st as ss, *skip 2 sts**, (3tr, ch2, 3tr) in next st*, rep from * to * 2x and * to ** 1x, 3tr in same st as first sts, ch1, join with dc to 3rd ch of stch. {6 sts on each side; 4 2-ch cnr sps}

R3: dc over joining dc, *dc in next 2 sts, spike dc over next 2 sts into next 2 sts of R1 below, dc in next 2 sts**, (dc, ch2, dc) in 2-ch sp*, rep from * to * 2x and * to ** 1x, dc in same sp as first st, ch1, join with dc to first st. {8 sts on each side; 4 2-ch cnr sps}

R4: ch3 (stch), tr over joining dc, *tr in next 8 sts**, (2tr, ch2, 2tr) in 2-ch sp*, rep from * to * 2x and * to ** 1x, 2tr in same sp as first sts, ch1, join with dc to 3rd ch of stch. {12 sts on each side; 4 2-ch cnr sps}

R5: dc over joining dc, *dc in next 5 sts, spike dc over next 2 sts into next 2 sts of R3 below, dc in next 5 sts**, (dc, ch2, dc) in 2-ch sp*, rep from * to * 2x and * to ** 1x, dc in same sp as first st, ch1, join with dc to first st. {14 sts on each side; 4 2-ch cnr sps}

R6: ch3 (stch), *tr in next 14 sts**, (tr, ch2, tr) in 2-ch sp*, rep from * to * 2x and * to ** 1x, tr in same sp as first st, ch1, join with dc to 3rd ch of stch. {16 sts on each side; 4 2-ch cnr sps}

R7: dc over joining dc, *dc in next 3 sts, 2x [spike dc over next 2 sts into next 2 sts of R5 below, dc in next 2 sts], spike dc over next 2 sts into next 2 sts of R5 below, dc in next 3 sts**, (dc, ch2, dc) in 2-ch sp*, rep from * to * 2x and * to ** 1x, dc in same sp as first st, ch1, join with dc to first st. {18 sts on each side; 4 2-ch cnr sps}

R8: ch3 (stch), *tr in next 18 sts**, (tr, ch2, tr) in 2-ch sp*, rep from * to * 2x and * to ** 1x, tr in same sp as first st, ch1, join with dc to 3rd ch of stch. {20 sts on each side; 4 2-ch cnr sps}

R9: dc over joining dc, *dc in next 20 sts**, (dc, ch2, dc) in next st*, rep from * to * 2x and * to ** 1x, dc in same sp as first st, ch2, join with ss to first st. Fasten off. {22 sts on each side; 4 2-ch cnr sps}

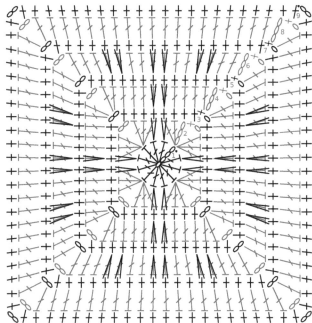

Bendigo Woollen Mills
Cotton 8 ply
1-2, 4, 6 and 8-9 Storm Cloud 827
3, 5 and 7 Latte 887

Cascade Ultra Pima
1-2 Turquoise 3733
3-4 Aqua 3732
5-6 Ice 3736
7-9 Natural 3718

Melbourne

 ⊙ 31m ✂

Attach yarn to hook with a slip knot, ch1, work all R1 sts into the 1-ch sp.

R1: ch4 (stch), *ch1, dtr, ch1**, dtr, ch3, dtr*, rep from * to * 2x and * to ** 1x, dtr, ch1, join with htr to 4th ch of stch. {3 sts, 2 1-ch sps on each side; 4 3-ch cnr sps}

R2: 2dc over joining htr, *2x [dc in next st, dc in 1-ch sp], dc in next st**, (2dc, ch2, 2dc) in 3-ch sp*, rep from * to * 2x and * to ** 1x, 2dc in same sp as first sts, ch1, join with dc to first st. {9 sts on each side; 4 2-ch cnr sps}

R3: ch3 (stch), *tr in next 9 sts**, (tr, ch2, tr) in 2-ch sp*, rep from * to * 2x and * to ** 1x, tr in same sp as first st, ch1, join with dc to 3rd ch of stch. {11 sts on each side; 4 2-ch cnr sps}

R4: dc over joining dc, *dc in next 11 sts**, (dc, ch2, dc) in 2-ch sp*, rep from * to * 2x and * to ** 1x, dc in same sp as first st, ch1, join with dc to first st. {13 sts on each side; 4 2-ch cnr sps}

R5: ch4 (stch), *6x [ch1, skip 1 st, dtr in next st], ch1, skip 1 st**, (dtr, ch3, dtr) in 2-ch sp*, rep from * to * 2x and * to ** 1x, dtr in same sp as first st, ch1, join with htr to 4th ch of stch. {8 sts, 7 1-ch sps on each side; 4 3-ch cnr sps}

R6: 2dc over joining htr, *7x [dc in next st, dc in 1-ch sp], dc in next st**, (2dc, ch2, 2dc) in 3-ch sp*, rep from * to * 2x and * to ** 1x, 2dc in same sp as first sts, ch1, join with dc to first st. {19 sts on each side; 4 2-ch cnr sps}

R7: ch3 (stch), *tr in next 19 sts**, (tr, ch2, tr) in 2-ch sp*, rep from * to * 2x and * to ** 1x, tr in same sp as first st, ch2, join with ss to 3rd ch of stch. Fasten off. {21 sts on each side; 4 2-ch cnr sps}

Julie's Melbourne
Scheepjes Cahlista
1 and 4 Red 390
2 Light Pink 222
3 Light Mint 385
5 Light Blue 397
6 Mid Green 389
7 Mid Blue 511
www.littlewoolliemakes.com.au

Cascade Ultra Pima
1-2 Turquoise 3733
3-4 Aqua 3732
5-6 Ice 3736
7 Natural 3718

To extend

Rep R4 to R7 as many times as needed, increasing the numbers as follows:

R4 "dc in next #+10 sts …" {#+10 sts …}

R5 "#+5x [ch1, skip …" {#+5 sts and #+5 1-ch sps …}

R6 "#+5x [dc in next …" {#+5 sts and #+5 1-ch sps …}

R7 "tr in next #+10 sts …" {#+10 sts}

Zahra

 40m

NOTES

• **R4:** the ch1 at the start is not included in the st count.

Begin with a mc or ch6 and join the last ch to the first with a ss to make a loop.

R1: ch3 (stch), *ch2, 3trcl, ch2**, tr*, rep from * to * 4x and * to ** 1x, join with ss to 3rd ch of stch.
{12 sts, 12 2-ch sps}

R2: dc in same st as ss, *2dc in 2-ch sp, skip 1 st, 2dc in 2-ch sp**, (dc, ch2, dc) in next st*, rep from * to * 4x and * to ** 1x, dc in same st as first st, ch1, join with dc to first st. {36 sts, 6 2-ch sps}

R3: ch3 (stch), 4tr over joining dc, *skip 3 sts, fpdc around R1 st below, skip 3 sts**, 9tr in 2-ch sp*, rep from * to * 4x and * to ** 1x, 4tr in same sp as first sts, join with ss to 3rd ch of stch. {60 sts}

R4: ch1, bpdc around same st ss was worked into, *ch4, skip 4 sts, fpdtr around next st, ch4, skip 4 sts**, bpdc around next st*, rep from * to * 4x and * to ** 1x, join with ss to first st. {12 sts, 12 4-ch sps}

R5: ch3 (stch), *ch2, 5trcl in 4-ch sp, ch2**, tr in next st*, rep from * to * 10x and * to ** 1x, join with ss to 3rd ch of stch. {24 sts, 24 2-ch sps}

R6: ch4 (stch), *(dtr, hdtr) in 2-ch sp, hdtr in next st, 2tr in 2-ch sp, htr in next st, (htr, dc) in 2-ch sp, dc in next st, (dc, htr) in 2-ch sp, htr in next st, 2tr in 2-ch sp, hdtr in next st, (hdtr, dtr) in 2-ch sp**, (dtr, ch3, dtr) in next st*, rep from * to * 2x and * to ** 1x, dtr in same sp as first st, ch1, join with htr to 4th ch of stch. {19 sts on each side; 4 3-ch cnr sps}

R7: dc over joining htr, *dc in next 19 sts**, (dc, ch2, dc) in 3-ch sp*, rep from * to * 2x and * to ** 1x, dc in same sp as first st, ch1, join with dc to first st.
{21 sts on each side; 4 2-ch cnr sps}

R8: dc over joining dc, *dc in next 21 sts**, (dc, ch2, dc) in 2-ch sp*, rep from * to * 2x and * to ** 1x, dc in same sp as first st, ch1, join with dc to first st.
{23 sts on each side; 4 2-ch cnr sps}

R9: dc over joining dc, *dc in next 23 sts**, (dc, ch2, dc) in 2-ch sp*, rep from * to * 2x and * to ** 1x, dc in same sp as first st, ch2, join with ss to first st. Fasten off.
{25 sts on each side; 4 2-ch cnr sps}

Michelle's Zahra
Cascade Ultra Pima
1 Honeysuckle 3802
2-3 Deep Coral 3767
4 Ice 3736
5 Cool Mint 3775
6 Natural 3718
7-9 Sunshine 3764
www.poppyandbliss.com

Cascade Ultra Pima
1-2 Turquoise 3733
3-4 Aqua 3732
5 Ice 3736
6-9 Natural 3718

Lazarev

  32m

NOTES

- It may be a bit ruffled until the end of R6.

Attach yarn to hook with a slip knot, ch1, work all R1 sts into the 1-ch sp.

R1: ch3 (stch), 7tr, join with ss to 3rd ch of stch. {8 sts}

R2: ch3 (stch), *ch3, dc in next st, ch3**, tr in next st*, rep from * to * 2x and * to ** 1x, join with ss to 3rd ch of stch. {8 sts, 8 3-ch sps}

R3: ch3 (stch), 2tr in same st as ss, *skip 3-ch sp, dc in next st, skip 3-ch sp**, (3tr, ch2, 3tr) in next st*, rep from * to * 2x and * to ** 1x, 3tr in same sp as first sts, ch1, join with dc to 3rd ch of stch. {7 sts on each side; 4 2-ch cnr sps}

R4: ch3 (stch), tr over joining dc, *2tr in next 3 sts, skip 1 st, 2tr in next 3 sts**, (2tr, ch2, 2tr) in 2-ch sp*, rep from * to * 2x and * to ** 1x, 2tr in same sp as first sts, ch1, join with dc to 3rd ch of stch. {16 sts on each side; 4 2-ch cnr sps}

R5: ch3 (stch), *tr in next 7 sts, fptr around next 2 sts at the same time, tr in next 7 sts**, (tr, ch2, tr) in 2 ch sp*, rep from * to * 2x and * to ** 1x, tr in same sp as first st, ch1, join with dc to 3rd ch of stch. {17 sts on each side; 4 2-ch cnr sps}

R6: dc over joining dc, *dc in next 7 sts, ch1, skip next 3 sts, dc in next 7 sts**, (dc, ch2, dc) in 2-ch sp*, rep from * to * 2x and * to ** 1x, dc in same sp as first st, ch1, join with dc to first st. {16 sts, 1 1-ch sp on each side; 4 2-ch cnr sps}

R7: ch3 (stch), *4x [ch1, skip 1 st, tr in next st], ch1, skip 1-ch sp, 4x [tr in next st, ch1, skip 1 st]**, (tr, ch3, tr) in 2-ch sp*, rep from * to * 2x and * to ** 1x, tr in same sp as first st, ch1, join with htr to 3rd ch of stch. {10 sts, 9 1-ch sps on each side; 4 3-ch cnr sps}

R8: 2dc over joining htr, *9x [dc in next st, dc in 1-ch sp], dc in next st**, (2dc, ch2, 2dc) in 3-ch sp*, rep from * to * 2x and * to ** 1x, 2dc in same sp as first sts, ch2, join with ss to first st. Fasten off. {23 sts on each side; 4 2-ch cnr sps}

Cascade Ultra Pima
1-3 Turquoise 3733
4 Aqua 3732
5-6 Ice 3736
7-8 Natural 3718

Paintbox Cotton DK
1-3, 5-6 and 8 Washed Teal 452
4 and 7 Lipstick Pink 433

Radius

  35m

NOTES

• **R1:** the ch1 at the start is not included in the st count.

Attach yarn to hook with a slip knot, ch1, work all R1 sts into the 1-ch sp.

R1: ch1, 8dc, join with ss to first st. {8 sts}

R2: ch3 (stch), tr in same st as ss, 2tr in next 7 sts, join with ss to 3rd ch of stch. {16 sts}

R3: ch3 (stch), tr in same st as ss, *tr in next st, fptr around st just worked into**, 2tr in next st*, rep from * to * 6x and * to ** 1x, join with ss to 3rd ch of stch. {32 sts}

R4: ch3 (stch), tr in next 3 sts, *fptr around st just worked into**, tr in next 4 sts*, rep from * to * 6x and * to ** 1x, join with ss to 3rd ch of stch. {40 sts}

R5: dc in same st as ss, dc in next 3 sts, *ch2, skip 1 st, dc in next 4 sts*, rep from * to * 6x, ch1, skip 1 st, join with dc to first st. {32 sts, 8 2-ch sps}

R6: ch3 (stch), 3tr over joining dc, *ch1, skip 4 sts**, 7tr in 2-ch sp*, rep from * to * 6x and * to ** 1x, 3tr in same sp as first sts, join with ss to 3rd ch of stch. {56 sts, 8 1-ch sps}

R7: dc in same st as ss, *ch6, skip (3 sts, 1-ch sp and 3 sts), dc in next st, ch6, skip (3 sts, 1-ch sp and 3 sts)**, (dc, ch2, dc) in next st*, rep from * to * 2x and * to ** 1x, dc in same st as first st, ch1, join with dc to first st.
{3 sts, 2 6-ch sps on each side; 4 2-ch cnr sps}

R8: ch4 (stch), hdtr over joining dc, *hdtr in next st, (2tr, 3htr, dc) in 6-ch sp, dc in next st, (dc, 3htr, 2tr) in 6-ch sp, hdtr in next st**, (hdtr, dtr, ch2, dtr, hdtr) in 2-ch sp*, rep from * to * 2x and * to ** 1x, (hdtr, dtr) in same sp as first sts, ch1, join with dc to 4th ch of stch.
{19 sts on each side; 4 2-ch cnr sps}

R9: dc over joining dc, *dc in next 19 sts**, (dc, ch2, dc) in 2-ch sp*, rep from * to * 2x and * to ** 1x, dc in same sp as first st, ch1, join with dc to first st.
{21 sts on each side; 4 2-ch cnr sps}

R10: dc over joining dc, *dc in next 21 sts**, (dc, ch2, dc) in 2-ch sp*, rep from * to * 2x and * to ** 1x, dc in same sp as first sts, ch2, join with ss to first st. Fasten off.
{23 sts on each side; 4 2-ch cnr sps}

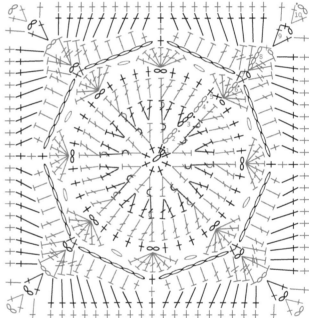

Paintbox Cotton DK
1 Rose Red 414
2 Blood Orange 420
3 Seville Orange 419
4-5 Buttercup Yellow 423
6 Daffodil yellow 422
7-10 Marine Blue 434

Cascade Ultra Pima
1-4 Turquoise 3733
5-6 Aqua 3732
7-8 Ice 3736
9-10 Natural 3718

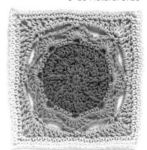

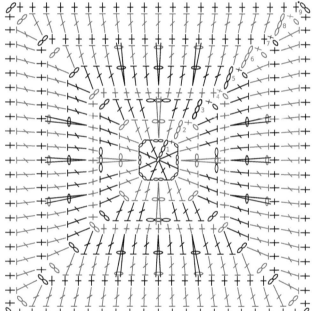

Bismarck

 40m

TIP

- Pull up very long loops when making the spike sts.

Attach yarn to hook with a slip knot, ch1, work all R1 sts into the 1-ch sp.

R1: ch3 (stch), *ch2, tr*, rep from * to * 6x, ch1, join with dc to 3rd ch of stch. {8 sts, 8 2-ch-sps}

R2: ch3 (stch), *tr in next st, ch2, skip 2-ch sp, tr in next st**, (tr, ch2, tr) in 2-ch sp*, rep from * to * 2x and * to ** 1x, tr in same sp as first st, ch1, join with dc to 3rd ch of stch. {4 sts, 1 2-ch sp on each side; 4 2-ch cnr sps}

R3: ch3 (stch), *tr in next 2 sts, ch3, skip 2-ch sp, tr in next 2 sts**, (tr, ch2, tr) in 2-ch sp*, rep from * to * 2x and * to ** 1x, tr in same sp as first st, ch1, join with dc to 3rd ch of stch. {6 sts, 1 3-ch sp on each side; 4 2-ch cnr sps}

R4: dc over joining dc, *dc in next 3 sts, dc in 3-ch sp, spike dc in 2-ch sp of R1 below, dc in 3-ch sp, dc in next 3 sts**, (dc, ch2, dc) in 2-ch sp*, rep from * to * 2x and * to ** 1x, dc in same sp as first st, ch1, join with dc to first st. {11 sts on each side; 4 2-ch cnr sps}

R5: ch3 (stch), *3x [tr in next 2 sts, ch1, skip 1 st], tr in next 2 sts**, (tr, ch2, tr) in 2-ch sp*, rep from * to * 2x and * to ** 1x, tr in same sp as first st, ch1, join with dc to 3rd ch of stch. {10 sts, 3 1-ch sps on each side; 4 2-ch cnr sps}

R6: ch3 (stch), *tr in next 3 sts, 2x [ch1, skip 1-ch sp, tr in next 2 sts], ch1, skip 1-ch sp, tr in next 3 sts**, (tr, ch2, tr) in 2-ch sp*, rep from * to * 2x and * to ** 1x, tr in same sp as first st, ch1, join with dc to 3rd ch of stch. {12 sts, 3 1-ch sps on each side; 4 2-ch cnr sps}

R7: dc over joining dc, *dc in next 4 sts, 2x [spike dc in skipped st of R4 below, dc in next 2 sts], spike dc in skipped st of R4 below, dc in next 4 sts**, (dc, ch2, dc) in 2-ch sp*, rep from * to * 2x and * to ** 1x, dc in same sp as first st, ch1, join with dc to first st.
{17 sts on each side; 4 2-ch cnr sps}

R8: ch3 (stch), *tr in next 17 sts**, (tr, ch2, tr) in 2-ch sp*, rep from * to * 2x and * to ** 1x, tr in same sp as first st, ch1, join with dc to 3rd ch of stch.
{19 sts on each side; 4 2-ch sp cnrs}

R9: dc over joining dc, *dc in next 19 sts**, (dc, ch2, dc) in 2-ch sp*, rep from * to * 2x and * to ** 1x, dc in same sp as first st, ch2, join with ss to first st. Fasten off.
{21 sts on each side; 4 2-ch sp cnrs}

To extend

Stop at the end of R7, rep R5 to R7 as many times as needed, increasing the numbers as follows:

R5 "#+2x [tr in next 2 sts ..." {#+4 sts, #+2 1-ch sps on ...}

R6 "#+2x [ch1, skip 1-ch sp ..." {#+4 sts, #+4 1-ch sps on ...}

R7 "#+2x [spike dc in skipped st of R#+3 ..." {#+6 sts on ...}

Then add R8 and R9.

Wool and the Gang Billie Jean
1-3, 5-6 and 8-9 Raw Denim
4 and 7 Washed Out Denim

Bendigo Woollen Mills
Cotton 4 ply
1-3, 5-6 and 8-9 Parchment 816
4 and 7 Kiwi 809

Cascade Ultra Pima
1-3 Turquoise 3733
4-6 Aqua 3732
7 Ice 3736
8-9 Natural 3718

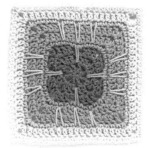

Bloem

 46m

NOTES

* **R2 and R6:** will be very ruffled.

Attach yarn to hook with a slip knot, ch1, work all R1 sts into the 1-ch sp.

R1: ch3 (stch), *ch4, tr*, rep from * to * 6x, ch4, join with ss to 3rd ch of stch. {8 sts, 8 4-ch loops}

R2: dc in same st as ss, *7tr in 4-ch sp**, dc in next st*, rep from * to * 6x, and * to ** 1x, join with ss to first st. {64 sts}

R3: dc in same st as ss, *ch2, skip 7 sts**, dc in next st*, rep from * to * 6x and * to ** 1x, join with ss to first st. {8 sts, 8 2-ch sps}

R4: ch2 (stch), *3htr in 2-ch sp**, htr in next st*, rep from * to * 6x and * to ** 1x, join with ss to 2nd ch of stch. {32 sts}

R5: ch2 (stch), ch4, htr in same st as ss, *skip 1 st, (htr, ch4, htr) in next st*, rep from * to * 14x, join with ss to 2nd ch of stch. {32 sts, 16 4-ch loops}

R6: dc between 2 sts below, *7tr in 4-ch sp**, dc between next 2 sts*, rep from * to * 14x and * to ** 1x, join with ss to first st. {128 sts}

R7: dc in same st as ss, *ch2, skip 7 sts**, dc in next st*, rep from * to * 14x and * to ** 1x, join with ss to first st. {16 sts, 16 2-ch sps}

R8: ch3 (stch), *2tr in 2-ch sp**, tr in next st*, rep from * to * 14x and * to ** 1x, join with ss to 3rd ch of stch. {48 sts}

R9: ch4 (stch), hdtr in same st as ss, *tr in next 2 sts, htr in next 2 sts, dc in next 3 sts, htr in next 2 sts, tr in next 2 sts**, (hdtr, dtr, ch2, dtr, hdtr) in next st*, rep from * to * 2x and * to ** 1x, (hdtr, dtr) in same sp as first sts, ch1, join with dc to 4th ch of stch. {15 sts on each side; 4 2-ch cnr sps}

R10: 2dc over joining dc, *dc in next 15 sts**, (2dc, ch2, 2dc) in 2-ch sp*, rep from * to * 2x and * to ** 1x, 2dc in same sp as first sts, ch1, join with dc to first st. {19 sts on each side; 4 2-ch cnr sps}

R11: dc over joining dc, *dc in next 19 sts**, (dc, ch2, dc) in 2-ch sp*, rep from * to * 2x and * to ** 1x, dc in same sp as first st, ch2, join with ss to first st. Fasten off. {21 sts on each side; 4 2-ch cnr sps}

Sarah's Bloem
Stylecraft Special XL
1 and 10 Cream 3055
2-3 Duck egg 1820
4-5 Sage 3056
6-7 Petrol 3059
8-9 and 11 Graphite 3060
www.annabooshouse.blogspot.com

Cascade Ultra Pima
1-3 Turquoise 3733
4-7 Aqua 3732
8-9 Ice 3736
10-11 Natural 3718

Posy

  34m

Begin with a mc or ch6 and join the last ch to the first with a ss to make a loop.

R1: ch3 (stch), 2tr, *ch2, 3tr*, rep from * to * 6x, ch1, join with dc to 3rd ch of stch. {24 sts, 8 2-ch sps}

R2: ch3 (stch), *ch2, tr3tog over next 3 sts, ch2**, tr in 2-ch sp*, rep from * to * 6x, and * to ** 1x, join with ss to 3rd ch of stch. {16 sts, 16 2-ch sps}

R3: ch3 (stch), *ch3, skip 2-ch sp, dc in next st, ch3, skip 2-ch sp, 5trcl in next st, ch3, skip 2-ch sp, dc in next st, ch3, skip 2-ch sp**, tr in next st*, rep from * to * 2x and * to ** 1x, join with ss to 3rd ch of stch.
{3 sts, 4 3-ch sps on each side; 4 1-st cnrs}

R4: ch3 (stch), *ch3, skip 3-ch sp, tr in next st, ch3, skip 3-ch sp, dc in next st, ch3, skip 3-ch sp, tr in next st, ch3, skip 3-ch sp**, (tr, ch2, tr) in next st*, rep from * to * 2x and * to ** 1x, tr in same st as first st, ch1, join with dc to 3rd ch of stch. {5 sts, 4 3-ch loops on each side, 4 2-ch cnr sps}

R5: ch3 (stch), *4x [tr in next st, 3tr in 3-ch sp], tr in next st**, (tr, ch2, tr) in 2-ch sp*, rep from * to * 2x and * to ** 1x, tr in same sp as first st, ch1, join with dc to 3rd ch of stch. {19 sts on each side, 4 2-ch cnr sps}

R6: ch3 (stch), *tr in next 19 sts**, (tr, ch2, tr) in 2-ch cnr sp*, rep from * to * 2x and * to ** 1x, tr in same sp as first st, ch1, join with dc to 3rd ch of stch.
{21 sts on each side; 4 2-ch cnr sps}

R7: dc over joining dc, *dc in next 21 sts**, (dc, ch2, dc) in next st*, rep from * to * 2x and * to ** 1x, dc in same sp as first st, ch2, join with ss to first st. Fasten off.
{23 sts on each side; 4 2-ch cnr sps}

Paintbox Cotton DK
1-2 and 7 Mandarin Orange 418
3-4 and 6 Melon Sorbet 417
5 Coffee Bean 411

Bendigo Woollen Mills
Cotton 8 ply
1 and 6 Daffodil 806
2-4 Honeydew 897
5 and 7 Kiwi 809

Cascade Ultra Pima
1-2 Turquoise 3733
3 Aqua 3732
4 Ice 3736
5-7 Natural 3718

Bellinghausen

  47m

Begin with a mc or ch4 and join the last ch to the first with a ss to make a loop.

R1: ch3 (stch), 15tr, join with ss to 3rd ch of stch. {16 sts}

R2: ch3 (stch), fptr around st ss'd into, fptr around next st, *ch3, fptr around next 2 sts, tr in same st last fp st was worked around**, ch2, tr in next st, fptr around same st last st was worked into, fptr around next st*, rep from * to * 2x and * to ** 1x, ch1, join with dc to 3rd ch of stch. {6 sts, 1 3-ch sp on each side; 4 2-ch cnr sps}

R3: ch3 (stch), *fptr around next 3 sts, ch4, skip 3-ch sp, fptr around next 3 sts**, (tr, ch2, tr) in 2-ch sp*, rep from * to * 2x and * to ** 1x, tr in same sp as first st, ch1, join with dc to 3rd ch of stch. {8 sts, 1 4-ch sp on each side; 4 2-ch cnr sps}

R4: ch3 (stch), *fptr around next 4 sts, ch5, skip 4-ch sp, fptr around next 4 sts**, (tr, ch2, tr) in 2-ch sp*, rep from * to * 2x and * to ** 1x, tr in same sp as first st, ch1, join with dc to 3rd ch of stch. {10 sts, 1 5-ch sp on each side; 4 2-ch cnr sps}

R5: ch3 (stch), *fptr around next 5 sts, ch2, dc over all 3-ch loops below, ch2, fptr around next 5 sts**, (tr, ch2, tr) in 2-ch sp*, rep from * to * 2x and * to ** 1x, tr in same sp as first st, ch1, join with dc to 3rd ch of stch. {13 sts, 2 2-ch sps on each side; 4 2-ch cnr sps}

R6: ch3 (stch), *fptr around next 3 sts, fptr3tog around next 3 sts, ch2, skip 2-ch sp, tr in next st, ch2, skip 2-ch sp, fptr3tog around next 3 sts, fptr around next 3 sts**, (tr, ch2, tr) in 2-ch sp*, rep from * to * 2x and * to ** 1x, tr in same sp as first st, ch1, join with dc to 3rd ch of stch. {11 sts, 2 2-ch sps on each side; 4 2-ch cnr sps}

R7: dc over joining dc, *fpdc around next 5 sts, 2dc in 2-ch sp, dc in next st, 2dc in 2-ch sp, fpdc around next 5 sts**, (dc, ch2, dc) in 2-ch sp*, rep from * to * 2x and * to ** 1x, dc in same sp as first st, ch1, join with dc to first st. {17 sts on each side; 4 2-ch cnr sps}

R8: ch3 (stch), *tr in next st, tr in next 5 sts of R6 behind R7 sts, htr in next 5 sts, tr in next 5 sts of R6 behind R7 sts, tr in next st**, (tr, ch2, tr) in 2-ch sp*, rep from * to * 2x and * to ** 1x, tr in same sp as first st, ch1, join with dc to 3rd ch of stch. {19 sts on each side; 4 2-ch cnr sps}

R9: ch2 (stch), *bphtr around next 19 sts**, (htr, ch2, htr) in 2-ch sp*, rep from * to * 2x and * to ** 1x, htr in same sp as first st, ch1, join with dc to 2nd ch of stch. {21 sts on each side; 4 2-ch cnr sps}

R10: dc over joining dc, *dc in next 21 sts**, (dc, ch2, dc) in 2-ch sp*, rep from * to * 2x and * to ** 1x, dc in same sp as first st, ch2, join with ss to first st. Fasten off. {23 sts on each side; 4 2-ch cnr sps}

Cascade Ultra Pima
1-3 Turquoise 3733
4-5 Aqua 3732
6-7 Ice 3736
8-10 Natural 3718

Bendigo Woollen Mills
Cotton 8 ply
1-7 Arctic 808
8-10 Snow 801

Valentina

  41m

Begin with a mc or ch4 and join the last ch to the first with a ss to make a loop.

R1: ch4 (stch), 3dtr, *ch3, 4dtr*, rep from * to * 2x, ch1, join with htr to 4th ch of stch.
{4 sts on each side; 4 3-ch cnr sps}

R2: ch4 (stch), *ch3, dtr4tog over next 4 sts, ch3**, (dtr, ch6, dtr) in 3-ch sp*, rep from * to * 2x and * to ** 1x, dtr in same sp as first st, ch2, join with tr to 4th ch of stch.
{3 sts, 2 3-ch sps on each side; 4 6-ch cnr sps}

R3: ch4 (stch), 4dtr over joining tr, *skip (1 st and 3-ch sp), dc in next st, skip (3-ch sp and 1 st)**, (5dtr, ch3, 5dtr) in 6-ch sp*, rep from * to * 2x and * to ** 1x, 5dtr in same sp as first sts, ch1, join with htr to 4th ch of stch.
{11 sts on each side; 4 3-ch cnr sps}

R4: dc over joining htr, *bphtr around next 3 sts, bptr around next 2 sts, bphdtr around next st, bptr around next 2 sts, bphtr around next 3 sts**, (dc, ch2, dc) in 3-ch sp*, rep from * to * 2x and * to ** 1x, dc in same sp as first st, ch1, join with dc to first st.
{13 sts on each side; 4 2-ch cnr sps}

R5: ch3 (stch), 4tr over joining dc, *skip 2 sts, dc in next st, skip 2 sts, 5tr in next st, skip 1 st, 5tr in next st, skip 2 sts, dc in next st, skip 2 sts**, (5tr, ch2, 5tr) in 2-ch space*, rep from * to * 2x and * to ** 1x, 5tr in same sp as first sts, ch1, join with dc to 3rd ch of stch.
{22 sts on each side; 4 2-ch cnr sps}

R6: dc over joining dc, *bphtr around next 3 sts, bptr around next 2 sts, bphdtr around next st, bptr around next 2 sts, bphtr around next 3 sts, dc between last st and next st, bphtr around next 3 sts, bptr around next 2 sts, bphdtr around next st, bptr around next 2 sts, bphtr around next 3 sts**, (dc, ch2, dc) in 2-ch sp*, rep from * to * 2x and * to ** 1x, dc in same sp as first st, ch1, join with dc to first st.
{25 sts on each side; 4 2-ch cnr sps}

R7: dc over joining dc, *dc in next 25 sts**, (dc, ch2, dc) in 2-ch sp*, rep from * to * 2x and * to ** 1x, dc in same sp as first st, ch2, join with ss to first st. Fasten off.
{27 sts on each side; 4 2-ch cnr sps}

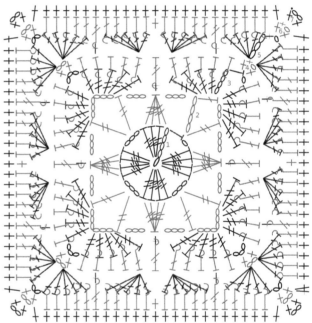

Bobbled

  -46m

NOTES

- R2, R5 and R8: will be ruffled.
- R3, R6 and R9: push the 5tr groups of sts forward from the back to create a bobble as you work the spike sts.

Attach yarn to hook with a slip knot, ch1, work all R1 sts into the 1-ch sp.

R1: ch3 (stch), 2tr, *ch2, 3tr*, rep from * to * 2x, ch1, join with dc to 3rd ch of stch.
{3 sts on each side; 4 2-ch cnr sps}

R2: ch3 (stch), *skip 1 st, 5tr in next st, skip 1 st**, (tr, ch2, tr) in 2-ch sp*, rep from * to * 2x and * to ** 1x, tr in same sp as first st, ch1, join with dc to 3rd ch of stch.
{7 sts on each side; 4 2-ch cnr sps}

R3: dc over joining dc, *dc in next st, spike dc in skipped st of R1 below, skip 2 sts, dc in next st, skip 2 sts, spike dc in skipped st of R1 below, dc in next st**, (dc, ch2, dc) in 2-ch sp*, rep from * to * 2x and * to ** 1x, dc in same sp as first st, ch1, join with dc to first st.
{7 sts on each side; 4 2-ch cnr sps}

R4: ch3 (stch), *tr in next 7 sts**, (tr, ch2, tr) in 2-ch sp*, rep from * to * 2x and * to ** 1x, tr in same sp as first st, ch1, join with dc to 3rd ch of stch.
{9 sts on each side; 4 2-ch cnr sps}

R5: ch3 (stch), *tr in next st, 3x [skip 1 st, 5tr in next st], skip 1 st, tr in next st**, (tr, ch2, tr) in 2-ch sp*, rep from * to * 2x and * to ** 1x, tr in same sp as first st, ch1, join with dc to 3rd ch of stch. {19 sts on each side; 4 2-ch cnr sps}

R6: dc over joining dc, *dc in next 2 sts, 3x [spike dc in skipped st of R4 below, skip 2 sts, dc in next st, skip 2 sts], spike dc in skipped st of R4 below, dc in next 2 sts**, (dc, ch2, dc) in 2-ch sp*, rep from * to * 2x and * to ** 1x, dc in same sp as first st, ch1, join with dc to first st.
{13 sts on each side; 4 2-ch cnr sps}

R7: ch3 (stch), *tr in next 13 sts**, (tr, ch2, tr) in 2-ch sp*, rep from * to * 2x and * to ** 1x, tr in same sp as first st, ch1, join with dc to 3rd ch of stch. {15 sts on each side; 4 2-ch cnr sps}

R8: ch3 (stch), *tr in next 2 sts, 5x [skip 1 st, 5tr in next st], skip 1 st, tr in next 2 sts**, (tr, ch2, tr) in 2-ch sp*, rep from * to * 2x and * to ** 1x, tr in same sp as first st, ch1, join with dc to 3rd ch of stch. {31 sts on each side; 4 2-ch cnr sps}

R9: dc over joining dc, *dc in next 3 sts, 5x [spike dc in skipped st of R7 below, skip 2 sts, dc in next st, skip 2 sts], spike dc in skipped st of R7 below, dc in next 3 sts**, (dc, ch2, dc) in 2-ch sp*, rep from * to * 2x and * to ** 1x, dc in same sp as first st, ch1, join with dc to first st. {19 sts on each side; 4 2-ch cnr sps}

R10: dc over joining dc, *dc in next 19 sts**, (dc, ch2, dc) in 2-ch sp*, rep from * to * 2x and * to ** 1x, dc in same sp as first st, ch2, join with ss to first st. Fasten off. {21 sts on each side; 4 2-ch cnr sps}

To extend

Stop at the end of R9, rep R7 to R9 as many times as needed, increasing the numbers as follows:

R7 "tr in next #+6 sts" {#+6 sts ...}

R8 "tr in next #+1 sts, #+2x [skip ... tr in next #+1 sts" {#+12 sts ...}

R9 "dc in next #+1 sts, #+2x [spike dc ... R#+3 ... skipped st of R#+ ... dc in next #+1 sts" {#+6 sts ...}

Then add R10.

Paintbox Cotton DK
1-2, 5 and 8 Washed Teal 433
3-4, 6-7 and 9-10 Banana Cream 421

Paintbox Cotton DK
1-2 and 7-8 Soft Fudge 410
3, 6 and 9 Vintage Pink 456
4-5 and 10 Coffee Bean 411

Cascade Ultra Pima
1-3 Turquoise 3733
4-6 Aqua 3732
7-9 Ice 3736
10 Natural 3718

Sibuyan

  37m

Begin with a mc or ch4 and join the last ch to the first with a ss to make a loop.

R1: ch3 (stch), tr around stch, *tr, tr around tr just made*, rep from * to * 6x, join with ss to 3rd ch of stch. {16 sts}

R2: ch3 (stch), tr around stch, *tr in next st, tr around tr just made*, rep from * to * 14x, join with ss to 3rd ch of stch. {32 sts}

R3: dc in same st as ss, dc in next 31 sts, join with ss to first st. {32 sts}

R4: *spike dc between sts of R2 below, ch2, skip 1 st*, rep from * to * 15x, join with ss to first st. {16 sts, 16 2-ch sps}

R5: ch3 (stch), *ch1, puff in 2-ch sp, ch1**, tr in next st*, rep from * to * 14x and * to ** 1x, join with ss to 3rd ch of stch. {32 sts, 32 1-ch sps}

R6: dc in same st as ss, *ch3, skip (1-ch sp, 1 st and 1-ch sp)**, dc in next st*, rep from * to * 14x and * to ** 1x, join with ss to first st. {16 sts, 16 3-ch sps}

R7: dc in same st as ss, *3dc in 3-ch sp**, dc in next st*, rep from * to * 14x and * to ** 1x, join with ss to first st. {64 sts}

R8: ch3 (stch), tr in same st as ss, *tr in next 2 sts, htr in next 3 sts, dc in next 5 sts, htr in next 3 sts, tr in next 2 sts**, (tr, hdtr, tr) in next st*, rep from * to * 2x and * to ** 1x, tr in same st as first sts, join with ss to 3rd ch of stch. {17 sts on each side; 4 1-st cnr sps}

R9: dc in same st as ss, *dc in next 17 sts**, (dc, ch2, dc) in next st*, rep from * to * 2x and * to ** 1x, dc in same st as first st, ch1, join with dc to first st. {19 sts on each side; 4 2-ch cnr sps}

R10: ch2 (stch), *htr in next 19 sts**, (htr, ch2, htr) in 2-ch sp*, rep from * to * 2x and * to ** 1x, htr in same sp as first st, ch2, join with ss to 2nd ch of stch. Fasten off. {21 sts on each side; 4 2-ch cnr sps}

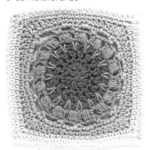

Cascade Ultra Pima
1-3 Turquoise 3733
4-5 Aqua 3732
6-8 Ice 3736
9-10 Natural 3718

Rachele's Sibuyan
Scheepjes Cahlista
1-2 Parrot Green 241
3 Apple Granny 513
4-5 Sky Blue 510
6-9 Cornflower 511
10 Petrol 400
www.cypresstextiles.net

Amaryllis

 34m

NOTES

- R2: the ch3 (stch) and 4trpc count as 1 5trpc.
- R4: the ch3 (stch) and the tr2tog count as 1 tr3tog.

Begin with a mc or ch6 and join the last ch to the first with a ss to make a loop.

R1: ch3 (stch), 23tr, join with ss to 3rd ch of stch. {24 sts}

R2: ch3 (stch), 4trpc in same st as ss, *ch2, skip 1 st, pc in next st*, rep from * to * 10x, ch2, join with ss to top of 4trpc. {12 sts, 12 2-ch sps}

R3: ss to next 2-ch sp, ch3 (stch), 2tr in same 2-ch sp, *skip 1 st, 3tr in 2-ch sp*, rep from * to * 10x, skip 1 st, join with ss to 3rd ch of stch. {36 sts}

R4: ch3 (stch), tr2tog over next 2 sts, *ch4, tr3tog over next 3 sts*, rep from * to * 10x, ch1, join with htr to top of tr2tog. {12 sts, 12 4-ch sps}

R5: ch4 (stch), (hdtr, tr) over joining htr, *tr in next st, 3htr in 4-ch sp, dc in next st, 3htr in 4-ch sp, tr in next st**, (tr, 2hdtr, ch2, 2hdtr, tr) in 4-ch sp*, rep from * to * 2x and from * to ** 1x, (tr, 2hdtr) in same sp as first sts, ch1, join with dc to 4th ch of stch.
{15 sts on each side; 4 2-ch cnr sps}

R6: ch3 (stch), tr over joining dc, *tr in next 15 sts**, (2tr, ch2, 2tr) in 2-ch sp*, rep from * to * 2x and from * to ** 1x, 2tr in same sp as first sts, ch1, join with dc to 3rd ch of stch.
{19 sts on each side; 4 2-ch cnr sps}

R7: ch2 (stch), *htr in next 19 sts**, (htr, ch2, htr) in 2-ch sp*, rep from * to * 2x and from * to ** 1x, htr in same sp as first st, join with ss to 2nd ch of stch. Fasten off.
{21 sts on each side; 4 2-ch cnr sps}

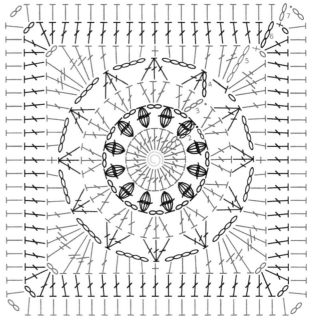

Mandy's Amaryllis 1
Paintbox Cotton DK
1 Daffodil Yellow 422
2 Bubblegum Pink 451
3-4 Peach Orange 455
5-7 Paper White 401
www.redagapeblog.com

Mandy's Amaryllis 2
Paintbox Cotton DK
1 Granite Grey 407
2 Bubblegum Pink 451
3-4 Lipstick Pink 452
5-7 Paper White 401
www.redagapeblog.com

Cascade Ultra Pima
1 Turquoise 3733
2 Aqua 3732
3-4 Ice 3736
5-7 Natural 3718

Vanes

  35m

Attach yarn to hook with a slip knot, ch1, work all R1 sts into the 1-ch sp.

R1: ch3 (stch), 7tr, join with ss to 3rd ch of stch. {8 sts}

R2: ch3 (stch), tr in same st as ss, *skip 1 st, (2tr, ch2, 2tr) in next st*, rep from * to * 2x, skip 1 st, 2tr in same st as first sts, ch1, join with dc to 3rd ch of stch.
{4 sts on each side; 4 2-ch cnr sps}

R3: ch3 (stch), tr over joining dc, *ch1, skip 2 sts, tr between previous and next st, ch1, skip 2 sts**, (2tr, ch2, 2tr) in 2-ch sp*, rep from * to * 2x and * to ** 1x, 2tr in same sp as first sts, ch1, join with dc to 3rd ch of stch.
{5 sts, 2 1-ch sps on each side; 4 2-ch cnr sps}

R4: ch3 (stch), tr over joining dc, *tr2tog over next 2 sts, ch1, skip 1-ch sp, (tr, ch2, tr) in next st, ch1, skip 1-ch sp, tr2tog over next 2 sts**, (2tr, ch2, 2tr) in 2-ch sp*, rep from * to * 2x and * to ** 1x, 2tr in same sp as first sts, ch1, join with dc to 3rd ch of stch.
{8 sts, 2 1-ch sps, 1 2-ch sp on each side; 4 2-ch cnr sps}

R5: ch3 (stch), tr over joining dc, *tr3tog over next 3 sts, ch1, skip (1-ch sp and 1 st), 7tr in 2-ch sp, ch1, skip (1 st and 1-ch sp), tr3tog over next 3 sts**, (2tr, ch2, 2tr) in 2-ch sp*, rep from * to * 2x and * to ** 1x, 2tr in same sp as first sts, ch1, join with dc to 3rd ch of stch.
{13 sts, 2 1-ch sps on each side; 4 2-ch cnr sps}

R6: ch3 (stch), tr over joining dc, *tr3tog over next 3 sts, ch5, skip (1-ch sp and 3 sts), dc in next st, ch5, skip (3 sts and 1-ch sp), tr3tog over next 3 sts**, (2tr, ch2, 2tr) in 2-ch sp*, rep from * to * 2x and * to ** 1x, 2tr in same sp as first sts, ch1, join with dc to 3rd ch of stch.
{7 sts, 2 5-ch sps on each side; 4 2-ch cnr sps}

R7: ch3 (stch), tr over joining dc, *tr in next 3 sts, 5tr in 5-ch sp, tr in next st, 5tr in 5-ch sp, tr in next 3 sts**, (2tr, ch2, 2tr) in 2-ch sp*, rep from * to * 2x and * to ** 1x, 2tr in same sp as first sts, ch1, join with dc to 3rd ch of stch.
{21 sts on each side; 4 2-ch cnr sps}

R8: dc over joining dc, *dc in next 21 sts**, (dc, ch2, dc) in next st*, rep from * to * 2x and * to ** 1x, dc in same sp as first st, ch2, join with ss to first st. Fasten off.
{23 sts on each side; 4 2-ch cnr sps}

Cascade Ultra Pima
1-3 Turquoise 3733
4-5 Aqua 3732
6 Ice 3736
7-8 Natural 3718

Sandra's Vanes
Rico Design Essentials Cotton
1 and 5 Beige
2 and 6-8 Orchid
3-4 Curry
www.mobiusgirldesign.com

Chicane

 ‑37m

Attach yarn to hook with a slip knot, ch1, work all R1 sts into the 1‑ch sp.

R1: ch3 (stch), tr, *ch4**, 3tr*, rep from * to * 2x and * to ** 1x, tr, join with ss to 3rd ch of stch. {12 sts, 4 4‑ch sps}

R2: dc in same st as ss, *ch3, skip 1 st, dc in 4‑ch sp, ch3, skip 1 st**, dc in next st*, rep from * to * 2x and * to ** 1x, join with ss to first st. {8 sts, 8 3‑ch sps}

R3: ch3 (stch), *2tr in 3‑ch sp, (tr, ch2, tr) in next st, 2tr in 3‑ch sp,**, tr in next st*, rep from * to * 2x and * to ** 1x, join with ss to 3rd ch of stch. {28 sts, 4 2‑ch sps}

R4: dc in same st as ss, *ch3, skip 1 st, dc in next st, ch3, skip 1 st, dc in 2‑ch sp*, ch3, skip 1 st, dc in next st, ch3, skip 1 st**, dc in next st, rep from * to * 2x and * to ** 1x, join with ss to first st. {16 sts, 16 3‑ch sps}

R5: ch3 (stch), *2tr in 3‑ch sp, tr in next st, 2htr in 3‑ch sp, dc in next st, 2htr in 3‑ch sp, tr in next st, 2tr in 3‑ch sp**, tr in next st*, rep from * to * 2x and * to ** 1x, join with ss to 3rd ch of stch. {48 sts}

R6: dc in same st as ss, *ch2, skip 1 st**, dc in next st*, rep from * to * 22x and * to ** 1x, join with ss to first st. {24 sts, 24 2‑ch sps}

R7: dc in same st as ss, *2dc in 2‑ch sp**, dc in next st*, rep from * to * 22x and * to ** 1x, join with ss to first st. {72 sts}

R8: ch4 (stch), 3dtr in same st as ss, *skip 3 sts, dc in next 11 sts, skip 3 sts**, 7dtr in next st*, rep from * to * 2x and * to ** 1x, 3dtr in same st as first sts, join with ss to 4th ch of stch. {11 sts on each side; 4 7‑st cnrs}

R9: dc in same st as ss, *8x [ch2, skip 1 st, dc in next st], ch2, skip 1 st**, (dc, ch2, dc) in next st*, rep from * to * 2x and * to ** 1x, dc in same sp as first st, ch1, join with dc to first st. {10 sts, 9 2‑ch sps on each side; 4 2‑ch cnr sps}

R10: dc over joining dc, *9x [dc in next st, dc in 2‑ch sp], dc in next st**, (dc, ch2, dc) in 2‑ch sp*, rep from * to * 2x and * to ** 1x, dc in same sp as first st, ch1, join with dc to first st. {21 sts on each side; 4 2‑ch cnr sps}

R11: dc over joining dc, *dc in next 21 sts**, (dc, ch2, dc) in next st*, rep from * to * 2x and * to ** 1x, dc in same sp as first st, ch2, join with ss to first st. Fasten off. {23 sts on each side; 4 2‑ch cnr sps}

Dedri's Chicane, Scheepjes Catona
1 Dark Turquoise 146
2‑3 Green Yellow 245
4‑5 Yellow 208
6‑7 Powder Pink 238
8 Tulip Pink 222
9‑10 Dark Pink 114
11 Cyan 397
www.lookatwhatimade.net

Cascade Ultra Pima
1‑3 Turquoise 3733
4‑5 Aqua 3732
6‑8 Ice 3736
9‑11 Natural 3718

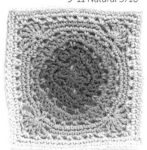

Pinkie

  37m

Begin with a mc or ch4 and join the last ch to the first with a ss to make a loop.

R1: ch3 (stch), 15tr, join with ss to 3rd ch of stch. {16 sts}

R2: dc in same st as ss, *ch3, dc in next st*, rep from * to * 14x, ch1, join with htr to first st. {16 sts, 16 3-ch sps}

R3: ch3 (stch), tr over joining htr, *skip 1 st, pc in 3-ch sp, skip 1 st**, 3tr in 3-ch sp*, rep from * to * 6x and * to ** 1x, tr in same sp as first sts, join with ss to 3rd ch of stch. {32 sts}

R4: ch3 (stch), *htr in next st, dc in sp between previous st and pc, dc in sp between pc and next st, htr in next st**, (tr, ch2, tr) in next st*, rep from * to * 6x and * to ** 1x, tr in same sp as first st, ch1, join with dc to 3rd ch of stch {48 sts, 8 2-ch sps}

R5: dc over joining dc, *ch3, dtr in top of pc from R3, ch3**, dc in 2-ch sp*, rep from * to * 6x and * to ** 1x, join with ss to first st. {16 sts, 16 3-ch sps}

R6: ch4 (stch), *(hdtr, 2tr) in 3-ch sp, htr in next st, (htr, 2dc) in 3-ch sp, dc in next st, (2dc, htr) in 3-ch sp, htr in next st, (2tr, hdtr) in 3-ch sp**, (dtr, ch2, dtr) in next st*, rep from * to * 2x and * to ** 1x, dtr in same st as first st, ch1, join with dc to 4th ch of stch. {17 sts on each side; 4 2-ch cnr sps}

R7: ch3 (stch), tr over joining dc, *tr in next 17 sts**, (2tr, ch2, 2tr) in 2-ch sp*, rep from * to * 2x and * to ** 1x, 2tr in same sp as first sts, ch1, join with dc to 3rd ch of stch. {21 sts on each side; 4 2-ch cnr sps}

R8: dc over joining dc, *dc in next 21 sts**, (dc, ch2, dc) in 2-ch sp*, rep from * to * 2x and * to ** 1x, dc in same sp as first st, ch2, join with ss to first st. Fasten off. {23 sts on each side; 4 2-ch cnr sps}

Cascade Ultra Pima
1-3 Turquoise 3733
4 Aqua 3732
5-6 Ice 3736
7-8 Natural 3718

Bendigo Woollen Mills Cotton 8 ply
1-2, 5-6 and 8 Pink Rose 805
3-4 and 7 Blush 811

King Cole Cottonsoft
1-2 Buttercup 1600
3-4 Cherry 719
5-6 and 8 Sage 1576
7 Lime 1601

Mozambique

  35m

Attach yarn to hook with a slip knot, ch1, work all R1 sts into the 1-ch sp.

R1: ch3 (stch), *ch1, tr*, rep from * to * 10x, ch1, join with ss to 3rd ch of stch. {12 sts, 12 1-ch sps}

R2: dc in same st as ss, *dc in 1-ch sp**, dc in next st*, rep from * to * 10x and * to ** 1x, join with ss to first st. {24 sts}

R3: ch3 (stch), tr in same st as ss, *skip 1 st**, 3tr in next st*, rep from * to * 10x and * to ** 1x, tr in same st as first sts, join with ss to 3rd ch of stch. {36 sts}

R4: dc in same st as ss, dc in next st, *dc between last and next st**, dc in next 3 sts*, rep from * to * 10x and * to ** 1x, dc in next st, join with ss to first st. {48 sts}

R5: ch3 (stch), *ch1, skip 1 st**, tr in next st*, rep from * to * 22x and * to ** 1x, join with ss to 3rd ch of stch. {24 sts, 24 1-ch sps}

R6: dc in same st as ss, *2dc in 1-ch sp, dc in next st, dc in 1-ch sp**, dc in next st*, rep from * to * 10x and * to ** 1x, join with ss to first st. {60 sts}

R7: ch3 (stch), tr in same st as ss, *skip 2 sts**, 3tr in next st*, rep from * to * 18x and * to ** 1x, tr in same st as first sts, join with ss to 3rd ch of stch. {60 sts}

R8: dc in same st as ss, dc in next st, *dc between previous and next sts**, dc in next 3 sts*, rep from * to * 18x and * to ** 1x, dc in next st, join with ss to first st. {80 sts}

R9: ch4 (stch), 2x [ch1, dtr] in same st as ss, *ch1, skip 3 sts, 6x [dc in next st, ch1, skip 1 st], dc in next st, ch1, skip 3 sts**, (dtr, 4x [ch1, dtr]) in next st*, rep from * to * 2x and * to ** 1x, 2x [dtr, ch1] in same st as first sts, join with ss to 4th ch of stch. {11 sts, 12 1-ch sps on each side; 4 1-st cnrs}

R10: dc in same st as ss, *11x [dc in 1-ch sp, dc in next st], dc in 1-ch sp**, (dc, ch2, dc) in next st*, rep from * to * 2x and * to ** 1x, dc in same st as first sts, ch2, join with ss to first st. Fasten off. {25 sts on each side; 4 2-ch cnr sps}

Scheepjes Catona
1-2 Hot Red 115
3 Tangerine 281
4-6 Yellow Gold 208
7-8 Kiwi 205
9-10 Vivid Blue 116

Cascade Ultra Pima
1-3 Turquoise 3733
4-6 Aqua 3732
7-8 Ice 3736
9-10 Natural 3718

Cogs

  31m

Attach yarn to hook with a slip knot, ch1, work all R1 sts into the 1-ch sp.

R1: ch3 (stch), *ch2**, tr*, rep from * to * 4x and * to ** 1x, join with ss to 3rd ch of stch. {6 sts, 6 2-ch sps}

R2: ch3 (stch), *3tr in 2-ch sp**, tr in next st*, rep from * to * 4x and * to ** 1x, join with ss to 3rd ch of stch. {24 sts}

R3: ch3 (stch), *ch3, skip 1 st**, tr in next st*, rep from * to * 10x and * to ** 1x, join with ss to 3rd ch of stch. {12 sts, 12 3-ch sps}

R4: ch3 (stch), *3tr in 3-ch sp**, tr in next st*, rep from * to * 10x and * to ** 1x, join with ss to 3rd ch of stch. {48 sts}

R5: ch3 (stch), *ch2, skip 1 st**, tr in next st*, rep from * to * 22x and * to ** 1x, join with ss to 3rd ch of stch. {24 sts, 24 2-ch sps}

R6: dc in same st as ss, *2dc in 2-ch sp**, dc in next st*, rep from * to * 22x and * to ** 1x, join with ss to first st. {72 sts}

R7: ch4 (stch), 3dtr in same st as ss, *skip 2 sts, dc in next 13 sts, skip 2 sts**, 7dtr in next st*, rep from * to * 2x and * to ** 1x, 3dtr in same st as first sts, join with ss to 4th ch of stch. {13 sts on each side; 4 7-st cnrs}

R8: dc in same st as ss, *dc in next 3 sts, htr in next st, tr in next 11 sts, htr in next st, dc in next 3 sts**, (dc, ch2, dc) in next st*, rep from * to * 2x and * to ** 1x, dc in same sp as first st, ch2, join with ss to first st. Fasten off. {21 sts on each side; 4 2-ch cnr sps}

Cascade Ultra Pima
1-2 Turquoise 3733
3-4 Aqua 3732
5-7 Ice 3736
8 Natural 3718

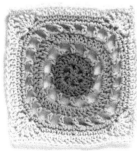

Bendigo Woollen Mills
Cotton 8 ply
1, 3 and 5 Daffodil 806
2, 4 and 6-8 Glacier 818

Jane's Cogs 1
Vinnis Colours Nikkim Cotton DK
1-2 Red
3-4 Pink
5-8 Ballet Pink
www.yarnbombersunited.weebly.com

Jane's Cogs 2
Scheepjes Cahlista
1, 3 and 5-8 Jade
2 Apple Granny
4 Cyan
www.yarnbombersunited.weebly.com

Banda

 33m

Attach yarn to hook with a slip knot, ch1, work all R1 sts into the 1-ch sp.

R1: ch3 (stch), 2tr, *ch2, 3tr*, rep from * to * 2x, ch1, join with dc to 3rd ch of stch.
{3 sts on each side, 4 2-ch cnr sps}

R2: dc over joining dc, *dc in next 3 sts**, (dc, ch2, dc) in 2-ch sp*, rep from * to * 2x and * to ** 1x, dc in same sp as first st, ch1, join with dc to first st.
{5 sts on each side; 4 2-ch cnr sps}

R3: ch3 (stch), tr over joining dc, *2x [tr in next st, ch1, skip 1 st], tr in next st**, (2tr, ch2, 2tr) in 2-ch sp*, rep from * to * 2x and * to ** 1x, 2tr in same sp as first sts, ch1, join with dc to 3rd ch of stch.
{7 sts, 2 1-ch sps on each side; 4 2-ch cnr sps}

R4: dc over joining dc, *dc in next 3 sts, dc in 1-ch sp, dc in next st, dc in 1-ch sp, dc in next 3 sts**, (dc, ch2, dc) in 2-ch sp*, rep from * to * 2x and * to ** 1x, dc in same sp as first st, ch1, join with dc to first st.
{11 sts on each side; 4 2-ch cnr sps}

R5: ch3 (stch), tr over joining dc, *tr in next st, ch3, skip 3 sts, tr in next 3 sts, ch3, skip 3 sts, tr in next st**, (2tr, ch2, 2tr) in 2-ch sp*, rep from * to * 2x and * to ** 1x, 2tr in same sp as first sts, ch1, join with dc to 3rd ch of stch.
{9 sts, 2 3-ch sps on each side; 4 2-ch cnr sps}

R6: dc over joining dc, *2x [dc in next 3 sts, 3dc in 3-ch sp], dc in next 3 sts**, (dc, ch2, dc) in 2-ch sp*, rep from * to * 2x and * to ** 1x, dc in same sp as first st, ch1, join with dc to first st. {17 sts on each side; 4 2-ch cnr sps}

R7: ch3 (stch), tr over joining dc, *tr in next st, ch1, skip 1 st, tr in next 2 sts, ch2, skip 2 sts, tr in next 5 sts, ch2, skip 2 sts, tr in next 2 sts, ch1, skip 1 st, tr in next st**, (2tr, ch2, 2tr) in 2-ch sp*, rep from * to * 2x and * to ** 1x, 2tr in same sp as first sts, ch1, join with dc to 3rd ch of stch.
{15 sts, 2 1-ch sps, 2 2-ch sps on each side; 4 2-ch cnr sps}

R8: dc over joining dc, *dc in next 3 sts, dc in 1-ch sp, dc in next 2 sts, 2dc in 2-ch sp, dc in next 5 sts, 2dc in 2-ch sp, dc in next 2 sts, dc in 1-ch sp, dc in next 3 sts**, (dc, ch2, dc) in 2-ch sp*, rep from * to * 2x and * to ** 1x, dc in same sp as first st, ch1, join with dc to first st.
{23 sts on each side; 4 2-ch cnr sps}

R9: dc over joining dc, *dc in next 23 sts**, (dc, ch2, dc) in 2-ch sp*, rep from * to * 2x and * to ** 1x, dc in same sp as first st, ch2, join with ss to first st. Fasten off.
{25 sts on each side; 4 2-ch cnr sps}

Paintbox Cotton DK
1-2 and 5-6 Royal Blue 441
3-4 and 7-9 Pillar Red 415

Cascade Ultra Pima
1-2 Turquoise 3733
3-4 Aqua 3732
5-6 Ice 3736
7-9 Natural 3718

Traverse

 37m

Attach yarn to hook with a slip knot, ch1, work all R1 sts into the 1-ch sp.

R1: ch3 (stch), 11tr, join with ss to 3rd ch of stch. {12 sts}

R2: ch3 (stch), fptr around st ss'd into, *tr in next st, fptr around next st, tr in st just worked around**, ch2, tr in next st, fptr around st just worked into*, rep from * to * 2x and * to ** 1x, ch1, join with dc to 3rd ch of stch. {5 sts on each side; 4 2-ch cnr sps}

R3: ch3 (stch), *2x [tr in next st, fptr around next st], tr in next st**, (tr, ch2, tr) in 2-ch sp*, rep from * to * 2x and * to ** 1x, tr in same sp as first st, ch1, join with dc to 3rd ch of stch. {7 sts on each side; 4 2-ch cnr sps}

R4: ch3 (stch), *tr in next 2 sts, fptr around next st, tr in next st, fptr around next st, tr in next 2 sts**, (tr, ch2, tr) in 2-ch sp*, rep from * to * 2x and * to ** 1x, tr in same sp as first st, ch1, join with dc to 3rd ch of stch. {9 sts on each side; 4 2-ch cnr sps}

R5: ch3 (stch), *tr in next 3 sts, fptr around next st, tr in next st, fptr around next st, tr in next 3 sts**, (tr, ch2, tr) in 2-ch sp*, rep from * to * 2x and * to ** 1x, tr in same sp as first st, ch1, join with dc to 3rd ch of stch. {11 sts on each side; 4 2-ch cnr sps}

R6: ch3 (stch), *tr in next 4 sts, fptr around next st, tr in next st, fptr around next st, tr in next 4 sts**, (tr, ch2, tr) in 2-ch sp*, rep from * to * 2x and * to ** 1x, tr in same sp as first st, ch1, join with dc to 3rd ch of stch. {13 sts on each side; 4 2-ch cnr sps}

R7: ch3 (stch), *tr in next 5 sts, fptr around next st, tr in next st, fptr around next st, tr in next 5 sts**, (tr, ch2, tr) in 2-ch sp*, rep from * to * 2x and * to ** 1x, tr in same sp as first st, ch1, join with dc to 3rd ch of stch. {15 sts on each side; 4 2-ch cnr sps}

R8: ch3 (stch), *tr in next 6 sts, fptr around next st, tr in next st, fptr around next st, tr in next 6 sts**, (tr, ch2, tr) in 2-ch sp*, rep from * to * 2x and * to ** 1x, tr in same sp as first st, ch1, join with dc to 3rd ch of stch. {17 sts on each side; 4 2-ch cnr sps}

R9: 2dc over joining dc, *dc in next 17 sts**, (2dc, ch2, 2dc) in 2-ch sp*, rep from * to * 2x and * to ** 1x, 2dc in same sp as first sts, ch2, join with ss to first st. Fasten off. {21 sts on each side; 4 2-ch cnr sps}

To extend

At the end of R8, rep R8 as many times as needed, increasing the numbers as follows:

R8 "tr in next #+1 ... tr in next #+1 sts" {#+2 sts ...}

Then add R9, working a st in each st on the side.

Cascade Ultra Pima
1-3 Turquoise 3733
4-6 Aqua 3732
7-8 Ice 3736
9 Natural 3718

Bendigo Woollen Mills
Luxury 8 ply
1, 3, 5, and 7 Curry 308
2, 4, 6, and 8-9 Sangria 351

Sol

 39m

NOTES

- R3 and R5: the ch1 at the start of these rounds are not included in the st count.

ch10, join with ss to first ch.

R1: ss over join into centre of 10-ch loop, ch3 (stch), 23tr in 10-ch loop, join with ss to 3rd ch of stch. {24 sts}

R2: fptr around st ss'd into, fptr around next 23 sts, join with ss to first st. {24 sts}

R3: ch1, tr in same st as ss join of R1, *2tr in next st of R1**, tr in next st of R1*, rep from * to * 10x and * to ** 1x, join with ss to first st. {36 sts}

R4: dc in same st as ss, ch2, dc in same st as ss join of R2, *ch2, skip 2 sts of R3**, dc in next st of R3, ch2, skip 1 st of R2, dc in next st of R2*, rep from * to * 10x and * to ** 1x, join with ss to first st. {24 sts, 24 2-ch sps}

R5: ch1, bpdc around same st as ss, *2tr in next st of R3, tr in next st of R3**, bpdc around next st*, rep from * to * 10x and * to ** 1x, join with ss to first st. {48 sts}

R6: dc in same st as ss, dc in next 47 sts, join with ss to first st. {48 sts}

R7: ch4 (stch), hdtr in same st as ss, *tr in next 2 sts, htr in next 2 sts, dc in next 3 sts, htr in next 2 sts, tr in next 2 sts**, (hdtr, dtr, ch2, dtr, hdtr) in next st*, rep from * to * 2x and * to ** 1x, (hdtr, dtr) in same st as first sts, ch1, join with dc to 4th ch of stch. {15 sts on each side; 4 2-ch cnr sps}

R8: dc over joining dc, *7x [ch3, skip 1 st, dc in next st], ch3, skip 1 st**, (dc, ch2, dc) in 2-ch sp*, rep from * to * 2x and * to ** 1x, dc in same sp as first st, ch1, join with dc to first st. {9 sts, 8 3-ch sps on each side; 4 2-ch cnr sps}

R9: ch3 (stch), tr over joining dc, *skip 1 st, dc in 3-ch sp, 7x [ch1, skip 1 st, dc in 3-ch sp], skip 1 st**, 3tr in 2-ch sp*, rep from * to * 2x and * to ** 1x, tr in same st as first sts, join with ss to 3rd ch of stch.
{8 sts, 7 1-ch sps on each side; 4 3-st cnrs}

R10: ch3 (stch), tr in same st as ss, *tr in next 2 sts, 7x [tr in 1-ch sp, tr in next st], tr in next st**, (2tr, ch2, 2tr) in next st*, rep from * to * 2x and * to ** 1x, 2tr in same sp as first sts, ch2, join with ss to 3rd ch of stch. Fasten off.
{21 sts on each side; 4 2-ch cnr sps}

Paintbox Cotton DK
1 Rose Red 414
2-3 Seville Orange 419
4-6 Buttercup Yellow 423
7-10 Kingfisher Blue 435

Cascade Ultra Pima
1-4 Turquoise 3733
5-6 Aqua 3732
7-9 Ice 3736
10 Natural 3718

 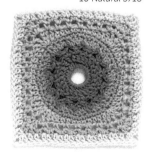

Projects

Now it's time to think of ways to use all these square patterns.

You can follow one of my projects or you can design your own using my pointers.

First up, I've eleven projects for you where everything you need to know is noted - the yarn and how much you'll need, the hook size and all the instructions to complete the project. They range from quick easy things like coasters, to big beautiful blankets, and some wearables too.

After my projects, you'll find some ideas and my tips on how to create your own projects.

Melbourne Wrap : Page 88

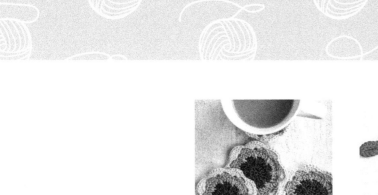

Radius Coasters : Page 82

Hot Shot Pot Holder : Page 83

Sunshine Cowl : Page 84

Dahlia Scarf : Page 85

Killarney Cushion Topper : Page 86

Deco Cushion : Page 87

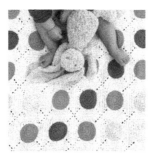

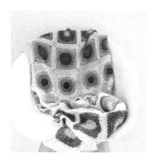

Cirque Baby Blanket : Page 90

Prism Lap Blanket : Page 92

Blossoming Flowers Blanket : Page 94

Heirloom Sampler Blanket : Page 96

Radius Coasters

What you'll make

4 coasters, 11 cm diameter

Yarn and amount

Yarn and Colours Must Have Minis
5ply/sport/baby mercerised cotton
1 ball = 10 grams/25 metres

A: 1 ball Anthracite (099), 8.5 grams used
B: 1 ball Shark Grey (096), 8.5 grams used
C: 1 ball Silver (094), 8.5 grams used

Hook size

3.5 mm

Pattern

Using the first 6 rounds of the Radius pattern on page 61, make 4 coasters.

R1-3 - A

R4-5 - B

R6 - C

Alter Round 6 as follows:

Attach C with ss to any 2-ch sp, ch3 (stch) (do not work false tr), 5tr in same sp, *ch1, skip 4 sts**, 7tr in 2-ch sp*, rep from * to * 6x and * to ** 1x, tr in same sp as first sts, join with inv join to first tr. Fasten off. {56 sts, 8 1-ch sps}

Hot Shot Pot Holder

What you'll make

1 hotpad/pot holder, 25 cm square

Yarn and amount

Bendigo Woollen Mills
10 ply/aran/worsted cotton
1 ball = 200 grams/360 metres

- 1 ball of French Navy (814), 210 metres used

Hook size

5 mm

Pattern

Using the D'Urville pattern on page 44, make 2 squares, extending the pattern.

Stop at the end of R7, rep R6 and R7 3x, increasing the numbers as follows:

R6 "... tr in next #+4 sts of R#+2" {#+4 sts ...}

R7 "... all R#+2, #+1x [..." {#+2 sts, #+1 2-ch sps ...}

Then add the following rounds:

R14: ch3 (stch), 2tr in same st as ss, *skip (R13 sts and ch sps), tr in next 24 sts of R12, 2tr in next st of R12**, 5tr in next st of R13*, rep from * to * 2x and * to ** 1x, 2tr in same sp as first sts, join with ss to 3rd ch of stch.
{26 sts on each side; 4 5-st cnrs}

R15: dc in same st as ss, *dc in next 2 sts of R14, 7x [2mtr in 2-ch sps of R13 and next sts of R14, dc in next 2 sts of R14]**, (dc, ch2, dc) in next st of R14*, rep from * to * 2x and * to ** 1x, dc in same sp as first st, ch1, join with dc to first st. {32 sts on each side; 4 2-ch cnr sps}

R16: dc over joining dc, *dc in next 32 sts**, (dc, ch2, dc) in 2-ch sp*, rep from * to * 2x and * to ** 1x, dc in same sp as first st, ch1, join with dc to first st.
{34 sts on each side; 4 2-ch cnr sps}

End the second square with ch1, join with dc to first st.

Hold squares wrong sides together, dc over joining dc and in 2-ch cnr sp of other square, *dc in next 34 sts of both squares**, 3dc in 2-ch cnr sps of both squares*, rep * to * 2x and * to ** 1x, dc in same 2-ch cnr sp as first st, ch12, skip 1 ch, dc in each of the 11 ch, turn, ss in next 11 sts, ss to first st of joining round, cut yarn and weave end to secure hanging loop. Fasten off.

Sunshine Cowl

What you'll make

1 cowl, 75 cm circumference and 15 cm wide

Yarn and amount

White Gum Wool Hand dyed By Briony
5ply/sport/baby 70% Tasmanian merino, 30% silk
1 skein = 100 grams/286 metres

- 1 skein of Sunshine, 230 metres used

Hook size

4 mm

Pattern

Using the Kruis pattern on page 51, make 5 squares.

Join the squares into a strip, then into a circular cowl using the zipper join.

Top and bottom edging

Working with the front face up, attach yarn with a ss to the blo of any st, ss in the blo of all sts along edge, join with inv join to first ss. Fasten off. Rep on other edge.

Dahlia Scarf

What you'll make

1 scarf, 22 cm wide and 160 cm long

Yarn and amount

Scheepjes Our Tribe
4 ply/fingering 70% merino superwash, 30% polyamide
1 ball = 100 grams/420 metres

• 2 balls Haak Maar Raak colour (963), 830 metres used

Hook size

3 mm

Pattern

Using the Dahlia pattern on page 36, make 30 squares.

Pattern Difference

Pull the magic circle tight.

Joining

Use the dc on back method to join the squares into 2 strips of 15 squares each, then join the strips to make a 15 x 2 rectangle.

Border

R1: Attach yarn with a stdg dc to any 2-ch cnr sp, *dc in each st on side, working a dc in each 2-ch sp and join**, (dc, ch2, dc) in 2-ch cnr sp*, rep from * to * 2x and from * to ** 1x, dc in same sp as first st, ch1, join with dc to first st.

R2: ch3 (stch), *tr in each st on side**, (tr, ch2, tr) in 2-ch cnr sp*, rep from * to * 2x and from * to ** 1x, tr in same sp as first st, ch2, join with ss to 3rd ch of st ch. Fasten off.

Killarney Cushion Topper

What you'll make

A 40 cm square cushion topper

Yarn and amount

Great Ocean Road Woollen Mill Loch Ard
8 ply/DK/light worsted 50/50 alpaca/Tarndie
polwarth wool
1 skein = 100 grams/158 metres

A: 1 skein of Granite, 140 metres used
B: 1 skein of Sandstone, 115 metres used

Hook size

5 mm

You'll also need a 40 cm ready-made cushion, sewing
thread and needle.

Pattern

Begin with A and change colours every 3 rounds,
alternating between A and B.

Using the Killarney Cross pattern on page 46, work R1 to
R6, then extend the pattern as follows:

Rep R6 12x, increasing the "... in next # sts ... in next #
sts**" by 2 and 2 each time. The stitch count will increase
by 4 each round.

R18 will have 69 sts on each side.

R19: Attach A with stdg dc to any 2-ch cnr sp, *dc in next
69 sts**, (dc, ch2, dc) in 2-ch cnr sp*, rep from * to * 2x
and * to ** 1x, dc in same sp as first st, ch2, join with ss to
first st. Fasten off. {71 sts on each side; 4 2-ch cnr sps}

Place square on front of cushion, hold in place using safety
pins at corners and the middle of the sides, hand sew to
cushion.

Deco Cushion

What you'll make

A large cushion, 46 cm square

Yarn and amount

Bendigo Woollen Mills
8 ply/DK/light worsted cotton
1 ball = 200 grams/485 metres

A: 1 ball Storm Cloud (827), 410 metres used
B: 1 ball Glacier (818), 180 metres used

Hook size

4 mm

You'll also need an 46 cm cushion insert or ready-made cushion.

Pattern

Square 1

Using the Deco pattern on page 22, make 5 circles in A and 4 circles in B, following instructions to the end of R4. Fasten off.

Work R5 and R6 to square off the circles. Attach squaring off colour to same stitch as ss with a stdg dtr. Square off the A circles using B and the B circles using A.

Arrange the 9 squares in a checkerboard layout as shown. Join the squares using A with the dc on front join.

Border

Attach A with a stdg dc to any 2-ch cnr sp, *dc in each st on side, working a dc in each 2-ch sp, ignoring the joins**, (dc, ch2, dc) in 2-ch cnr sp*, rep from * to * 2x and * to ** 1x, dc in same sp as first st, ch2, join with ss to first st.
{69 sts on each side; 4 2-ch cnr sps}

Square 2

Make one large square to 46 cm by extending the Deco pattern as follows:

Replace R6 with: ch4 (stch), dtr in same 2-ch sp, *dtr in next 19 sts**, (2dtr, ch2, 2dtr) in 2-ch cnr sp*, rep from * to * 2x and * to ** 1x, 2dtr in same sp as first st, ch1, join with dc to 4th ch of stch. {23 sts on each side; 4 2-ch cnr sps}

Rep R6 8x, increasing the "... in next # sts**" by 4 each time. The stitch count will increase by 4 each round.

R14 will have 55 sts on each side.

R15: 2dc over joining dc, *dc in next 55 sts**, (2dc, ch2, 2dc) in 2-ch sp*, rep from * to * 2x and * to ** 1x, 2dc in same sp as first st, ch2, join with ss to first st. Fasten off.
{59 sts on each side; 4 2-ch cnr sps}

Block both large squares.

Assembling the cushion

Square 1 will have 69 sts on each side and Square 2 will have 59 sts on each side.

Hold the 2 large squares wrong sides together. Attach A with a stdg dc to 2-ch cnr sps of both squares, dc in same 2-ch cnr sps, *9x [dc in both sts of both squares through both loops of next 6 sts, dc in same st on Square 2 just worked and next st of Square 1], dc in both sts of both squares through both loops of next 5 sts, dc in same st on Square 1 just worked and next st of Square 2**, 3dc in 2-ch cnr sps of both squares*, rep from * to * 2x, insert cushion insert, rep from * to ** 1x, dc in same sp as first st, join with ss to first st. Fasten off.
{69 sts on each side; 4 3-st cnrs}

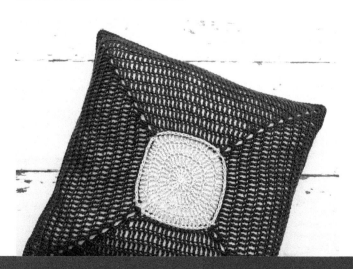

Melbourne Wrap

What you'll make

A shawl/wrap, 188 cm long x 47 cm wide

Yarn and amount

Scheepjes Our Tribe
4 ply/fingering 70% merino superwash, 30% polyamide
1 ball = 100 grams/420 metres

• 4 balls Lilla Bjorn colour (969), 1575 metres used

Hook size

3 mm

Pattern

Step 1

Using the Melbourne pattern on page 58, make 32 squares.

Join the squares into an 8 x 4 rectangle using the dc on back join.

Step 2

Make 2 large squares, extending the Melbourne Pattern by repeating R4 to R7 7x.

The numbers in each round will increase as follows:

R4: increasing the "… in next # sts**" by 10 sts each time. The stitch count will also increase by 10 each time.

R5: increasing the "#x [ch1, skip …" by 5 each time. The stitch and chain space counts will increase by 5 each time.

R6: increasing the "#x [dc in next st …" by 5. The stitch count will increase by 10 each time.

R7: increasing the "… in next # sts**" by 10 sts each time. The stitch count will also increase by 10 each time.

R35: end with ch2, join with ss to 3rd ch of stch. This round will have 91 sts on each side.

Joining

Note: Use the 2-ch sps and joins of the rectangle made with small squares when joining to the larger squares.

Join the squares together using the dc on back join accommodating the stitch count difference of 4 sts evenly as you join, with the rectangle made of small squares in the middle and the 2 large squares on either end.

Border

R1: Attach yarn with a stdg dc to any 2-ch cnr sp, *dc in each st on side, working a dc in each 2-ch sp and join**, (dc, ch2, dc) in 2-ch cnr sp*, rep from * to * 2x and from * to ** 1x, dc in same sp as first st, ch2, join with ss to first st.

Fringe

Cut 190 lengths of yarn 20 cm long and using crochet hook, attach one strand to each st and 2-ch cnr sp on short edges.

Insert your hook into the end st, fold the length of yarn in half and pull the middle of the yarn through with your hook, then pull both ends through the loop. Pull tight.

Cirque Baby Blanket

What you'll make

A baby blanket, 96 cm wide and 130 cm long

Yarn and amount

Bendigo Woollen Mills
4 ply/fingering cotton
1 ball = 200 grams/670 metres

R: 1 ball Pomegranate (819), 170 metres used
O: 1 ball Peach (807), 170 metres used
Y: 1 ball Daffodil (806), 170 metres used
G: 1 ball Honeydew (897), 170 metres used
B: 1 ball Sky (812), 170 metres used
P: 3 balls Parchment (816), 1,620 metres used

Hook size

3 mm

Pattern

Using the Cirque pattern on page 38, make 14 circles of each colour following instructions for R1 to R4. Square off each circle using P following instructions for R5 to R7.

Joining

Refer to chart for layout. Join using P and the dc on back join.

Border Pattern

R1: Attach P with a stdg dc to any 2-ch cnr sp, *dc in each st on side, working a dc in each 2-ch sp and join**, (dc, ch2, dc) in 2-ch cnr sp*, rep from * to * 2x and from * to ** 1x, dc in same sp as first st, ch1, join with dc to st.

R2: dc over joining dc, *dc in each st on side**, (dc, ch2, dc) in 2-ch cnr sp*, rep from * to * 2x and from * to ** 1x, dc in same sp as first st, ch2, join with ss to first st. Fasten off.

R3: Attach B with a stdg dc to any 2-ch cnr sp, *dc in each st on side**, (dc, ch2, dc) in 2-ch cnr sp*, rep from * to * 2x and from * to ** 1x, dc in same sp as first st, ch2, join with ss to first st. Fasten off.

R4: Rep R3 with P.

R5: Rep R3 with G.

R6: Rep R3 with P.

R7: Rep R3 with Y.

R8: Rep R3 with P.

R9: Rep R3 with O.

R10: Rep R3 with P.

R11: Rep R3 with R.

R12: Rep R3 with P.

R13: Rep R2 with P.

R	O	Y	G	B	R	O
O	Y	G	B	R	O	Y
Y	G	B	R	O	Y	G
G	B	R	O	Y	G	B
B	R	O	Y	G	B	R
R	O	Y	G	B	R	O
O	Y	G	B	R	O	Y
Y	G	B	R	O	Y	G
G	B	R	O	Y	G	B
B	R	O	Y	G	B	R

Prism Lap Blanket

What you'll make

A blanket, 115 cm square

Yarn and amount

Paintbox Yarns
8 ply/DK/light worsted cotton
1 ball = 50 grams/125 metres

R: 2 balls Tomato Red (413), 175 metres used
O: 2 balls Mandarin Orange (418), 175 metres used
Y: 2 balls Daffodil Yellow (422), 175 metres used
G: 2 balls Grass Green (430), 175 metres used
B: 2 balls Kingfisher Blue (435), 175 metres used
I: 2 balls Royal Blue (441), 175 metres used
V: 2 balls Rich Mauve (4445), 175 metres used
W: 7 balls Washed Teal (433), 780 metres used

Hook size

4 mm

Pattern

Using the Corona pattern on page 35, change colours as below:

R1-2: Colour 1

R3-4: Colour 2

R5: Colour 3

R6-7: Colour 4

R8-9: Colour 5

Make 49 squares, 7 in each of these colour ways:

1:	R - O - Y - G - W
2:	O - Y - G - B - W
3:	Y - G - B - I - W
4:	G - B - I - V - W
5:	B - I - V - R - W
6:	I - V - R - O - W
7:	V - R - O - Y - W

Joining

Refer to chart for layout. Join using W and the dc on back join.

Border

R1: Attach W with a stdg dc to any 2-ch cnr sp, *dc in each st on side, working a dc in each 2-ch sp and join**, (dc, ch2, dc) in 2-ch cnr sp*, rep from * to * 2x and * to ** 1x, dc in same sp as first st, ch1, join with dc to first st.

R2: ch3 (stch), *tr in each st on side**, (tr, ch2, tr) in 2-ch cnr sp*, rep from * to * 2x and * to ** 1x, tr in same sp as first st, ch1, join with dc to 3rd ch of stch.

R3: dc over joining dc, *(ch3, skip 1 st, dc) along side, ch3, skip last st**, dc in 2-ch cnr sp*, rep from * to * 2x and * to ** 1x, join with ss to first st. Fasten off.

5	5	5	5	5	5	5
6	6	6	6	6	6	6
7	7	7	7	7	7	7
1	1	1	1	1	1	1
2	2	2	2	2	2	2
3	3	3	3	3	3	3
4	4	4	4	4	4	4

Blossoming Flowers Blanket

What you'll make

A floral blanket, 117 cm square

Yarn and amount

King Cole Cottonsoft
8 ply/DK/light worsted cotton
1 ball = 100 grams/210 metres

B: 1 ball Buttercup (1600), 130 metres used
P: 1 ball Hot Pink (1848), 110 metres used
R: 1 ball Rose (1577), 90 metres used
C: 1 ball Cherry (719), 115 metres used
O: 1 ball Orchid (3033), 115 metres used
V: 1 ball Violet (717), 110 metres used
S: 2 balls Sage (1576), 420 metres used
L: 5 balls Lime (1601) , 930 metres used

Hook size

4 mm

Pattern

Use the Bloem (page 64), Bulaklak (page 52),
Pinkie (page 74) and Solomon (page 50) patterns.

Make:

12 Bloem - 2x C, 2x O, 2x P, 3x R, 3x V

9 Bulaklak - 2x C, 2x O, 2x P, 1x R, 2x V

20 Pinkie - 4x C, 4x O, 4x P, 4x R, 4x V

8 Solomon - 2x C, 2x O, 1x P, 2x R, 1x V

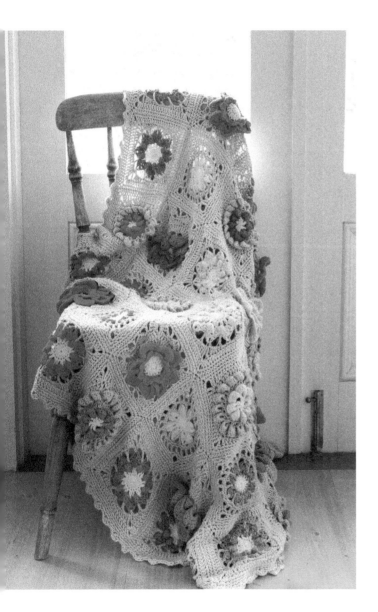

Change colours at these rounds:

BLOEM

R1: B

R2-3: C, O, P, R or V

R4-7: S

R8-11: L

PINKIE

R1-3: B

R4: C, O, P, R or V

R5-6: S

R7-8: L

BULAKLAK

R1-3: B

R4-6: C, O, P, R or V

R7-10: S

R11-12: L

SOLOMON

R1-2: B

R3: C, O, P, R or V

R4-7: S

R8-10: L

Joining

Refer to chart for layout. Join using L and the dc on back join. Bloem and Bulaklak have 21 sts on each side, whereas Pinkie and Solomon have 23 sts. When joining a 23 st square to a 21 st square, use the same stitch twice on the 21 st square, once near the start and once near the end of joining.

Border Pattern

R1: Attach L with a stdg dc to any 2-ch cnr sp, *dc in each st on side, working a dc in each 2-ch sp and join**, (dc, ch2, dc) in 2-ch cnr sp*, rep from * to * 2x and from * to ** 1x, dc in same sp as first st, ch1, join with dc to first st.

R2: dc over joining dc, *dc in each st on side**, (dc, ch2, dc) in 2-ch cnr sp*, rep from * to * 2x and from * to ** 1x, dc in same sp as first st, ch1, join with dc to first st.

R3: dc over joining dc, *dc in next 2 sts, 35x [skip 1 st, tr in next st, (htr, 2tr) around st just made, dc in next 3 sts]**, (dc, ch2, dc) in 2 ch sp*, rep from * to * 2x and * to ** 1x, dc in same sp as first st, ch2, join with ss to first st. Fasten off.

Layout

Blo C	Pin C	Pin C	Blo C	Pin V	Pin V	Blo V
Pin C	Bul C	Sol C	Bul V	Sol R	Bul V	Pin V
Pin C	Sol C	Blo R	Pin R	Blo V	Sol V	Pin V
Blo O	Bul C	Pin R	Bul R	Pin R	Bul P	Blo V
Pin O	Sol R	Blo R	Pin R	Blo R	Sol P	Pin P
Pin O	Bul O	Sol O	Bul O	Sol P	Bul P	Pin P
Blo O	Pin O	Pin O	Blo P	Pin P	Pin P	Blo P

Heirloom Sampler Blanket

What you'll make

A blanket, 135 cm x 114 cm

Yarn and amount

Bendigo Woollen Mills
8 ply/DK/light worsted cotton
1 ball = 200 grams/486 metres

- 5 balls Parchment (816), 2,310 metres used

Hook size

4 mm

Pattern

Make 1 of each of the 50 patterns. Make 6 patterns a second time - choose your favourites.

Arrange the 56 squares in a 7 x 8 grid and join using dc on back join. Order is not important. I placed the more solid squares on the edges and lacier ones inside the outer round.

Add the Simple Border explained in the Finishing Tips section.

Design your own projects

Crochet squares can be used in countless ways. I've given you a few projects, but you can do so many other things.

Follow these steps to come up with your own projects using the patterns in this book.

Decide what you want to make

Here are a few ideas to get you started:

- Use my projects as a guide, changing the patterns used to the ones you like.
- Make a strip of square bunting to decorate your space.
- Scarves and cowls are a simple way to get a taste for a pattern or two.
- Cushions are quick, easy projects.
- Blankets are a great choice and can be really fun. You can make a small blanket for a new baby, a lap blanket to keep you warm at your desk in winter, a snuggle blanket for the couch, all the way up to a king size bedspread.
- The great thing about a blanket is you can make it any size at all. If it's for a bed, decide if you want it to hang over the edges or sit on top. It can be any size that pleases you.

Choose pattern/s and layout

Once you've decided what you're going to make, you'll have a bit of planning to do so you can estimate how much yarn you'll need.

Use grid paper or create a table of squares on your computer to map out your layout. Once you've chosen your pattern/s, this will help decide how many of each square you'll need to make.

Now it's time to choose which patterns you'll use for your project. Here are just a few of the possibilities. I am sure you can come up with many more options as well.

- Use one pattern but use a different colour for each square.

- Use two or more squares of a similar theme or shape. Perhaps a few of the different circle to square patterns, or floral squares.

- Use contrasting squares. Maybe a solid square with a lacy one, or fancy and plain.

- Using just one square in several different colour ways is a great way to use up leftover bits and bobs of yarn as a stash busting project.

- Use one pattern with the same colour progression for every square.

- Use many or all of the patterns in the same colour way for each.

- Use one pattern but make each square in 2 colours, alternating the order.

- Choose a repeating pattern marked with the infinity symbol and, like the traditional granny square blanket, keep going to make a large square blanket. This is shown in the Melbourne Shawl and Killarney Cushion Topper projects.

Choose your yarn

Choose a yarn that suits your personal preference, budget and purpose. Consider trying a thinner or bulkier yarn than 8 ply/DK/light worsted for a completely different look.

Choose your hook

Don't be afraid to try a hook size other than what is recommended for your yarn. Experiment and see which end result you like best.

Choose your colours

Use the colours that make you happy. You're not bound by where I've changed colour. Mix it up and find combinations that please you.

Calculate yardage

The yardage stated for each pattern is for 8 ply/DK/ light worsted yarn made in a single colour using a 4 mm hook. Using a different yarn and/or hook will change the amount of yarn required.

Once you have decided what yarn, hook and colours you're going to use, make a sample square using your yarn of choice. Then use one of the following methods to see how much yarn you need for one square.

Method 1 - Weight

Calculate how many metres of yarn in 1 gram.

> e.g. a 200 gram ball of BWM 8 ply cotton is 485 metres, so, 485 divided by 200 equals 2.43 metres per gram.

> e.g. a 200 gram ball of BWM 4 ply cotton is 670 metres, so, 670 divided by 200 equals 3.35 metres per gram.

Make your square in your chosen colours. Using accurate scales that measure to 1 gram at least, weigh the square as you finish each colour, noting the weight.

> e.g. R1 to R2 of colour 1 = 4 grams. R3 to R4 of colour 2 = 9 grams. So you need 4 grams of colour 1 and 5 grams of colour 2 for one square. Calculate how much of each colour you used for the whole square.

Multiply the grams for each colour by your 1 gram calculation.

> e.g. Using the BWM 8 ply cotton, I'd multiply 2.43 x 4 to work out how much I needed to complete R1 to R2. So I would need 9.72 metres of that colour for each square. Repeat this for each colour used in your square.

Method 2 - Measure

Make a square using your chosen colours, but do not weave in the ends.

Unravel the square and measure each colour by measuring 1 metre then folding it on itself until you have a shorter length remaining. Count the number of 1-metre strands and measure the shorter length, adding that to your metres calculation.

Calculate your total yarn needs

No matter which method you use, the next step is to work out how much yarn you need for your whole project. Once you know how much yarn of each colour is required for one square, it's a simple matter of multiplying your results by the number of squares you need for your project. Repeat this process if you're using different square patterns.

Allow extra yarn for joining your project and adding a border. As an example, the Heirloom Sampler Blanket needed an extra 350 metres approximately to join and add the simple border.

Glossary

This list describes all the abbreviations, stitches and techniques used in this book. Abbreviations are simply words that have been shortened. Stitches are complete stitches you'll need to know. Techniques describe how particular stitches are made. Rather than explain all the variations that occur with these things combined, each abbreviation, stitch and technique is described on its own. You'll combine them all to create your squares.

It also shows the symbols used in the charts where applicable.

Abbreviations

	lge	large	
	R	round	
	rep	repeat	
	sml	small	
	sp/s	space/s	
	st/s	stitch/es	
	stch	starting chain	Used in place of the first st in a round. Is included in stitch count.
$\top_+$ $\complement_+$ $+_+$	stdg	standing	Attach yarn to your hook with a slip knot then work the stitch indicated as normal.
	yo	yarn over	Wrap yarn over hook from back to front.

Stitches

•	ss	slip stitch	Insert hook into st or sp indicated, yo and pull through st or sp and loop on hook.
o	ch	chain	Yarn over, pull through loop on hook.
+	dc	double crochet	Insert hook into st or sp indicated, yo, pull loop to front, yo, pull through both loops on hook.
T	htr	half treble crochet	Wrap yarn around hook, insert hook into st or sp indicated, yo, pull loop to front (3 loops on hook), yo, pull through all 3 loops on hook.
$\mathsf{\bar{T}}$	tr	treble crochet	Wrap yarn around hook, insert hook into st or sp indicated, yo, pull loop to front (3 loops on hook), 2x [yo, pull through 2 loops on hook].
$\mathsf{(\!f}$	mtr	modified treble crochet	Wrap yarn around hook, insert hook in st or sp indicated, pull loop to front (3 loops on hook), yo, pull through 2 loops, insert your hook in the st behind from the previous round and pull a loop to the front and through both loops on the hook.
$\mathsf{\bar{\bar{T}}}$	hdtr	half double treble crochet	Wrap yarn around hook twice, insert hook into st or sp indicated, yo, pull loop to front (4 loops on hook), yo, pull through 2 loops (3 loops on hook), yo, pull through all 3 loops on hook.
$\mathsf{\bar{\bar{T}}}$	dtr	double treble crochet	Wrap yarn around hook twice, insert hook into st or sp indicated, yo, pull loop to front (4 loops on hook), 3x [yo, pull through 2 loops].

Techniques

⌒	blo	back loop only	Insert hook into the back loop only of the st indicated.
⌣	flo	front loop only	Insert hook into the front loop only of the st indicated.
	bp	back post	Insert hook around the post of the st indicated from the back.
	fp	front post	Insert hook around the post of the st indicated from the front.
	cl	cluster	Numerous sts worked together in the same st or sp. Could be any number of any kind of st. e.g. 4trcl, 5dtrcl, 3htrcl.
	inv join	invisible join	Cut yarn after completing last st of round. Pull tail up through the last st, thread tail onto needle, insert needle under "v" of first true st of the round and back through the centre of the last st, and through the lbv of the last st. Pull tight enough to form a "v" on top of the stch, weave end away.
	lbv	loop behind v	The third loop or back bump of a st on the back. It's located under the back loop of a st.
	mc	magic circle	Method used to begin a square. Wrap yarn around a few fingers, forming a loop, insert your hook into the centre and pull the working yarn through, ch1 to secure. Work R1 sts into the ring, pull the tail to close the ring once all sts have been made and secure by weaving the end in well.
	pc	popcorn	A group of sts worked in the same st or sp, gathered together once all sts are made by removing hook, inserting it into the first st of the group and joining it to the last st of the group with a ss. If not specified, 5tr sts are used to make a pc. Otherwise, the number of sts required will be stated. e.g. 4trpc, 3trpc.
	picot	picot stitch	ch3, ss into first ch.
	puff	puff stitch	Insert hook into st or sp indicated, 5x [yo, pull loop to front] (11 loops on hook), yo, pull through all loops on hook.
	spike	spike st	Insert hook into st or sp indicated, usually in a round more than 1 round prior to the current round, pull up a long loop level with the current round and work st as normal. Can be any st e.g. spike dc, spike tr.
	tog	together	Numerous sts worked together. Work the specified number of sts up to just before the last step, end with a yo and pull through all loops on hook. "tog" will be followed by "over next # sts". It can be done with different numbers and types of sts. e.g. tr5tog over next 5 sts, dc2tog over next 2 sts.

Yarn Information

Yarns Used

Bendigo Woollen Mills Cotton and Wool
www.bendigowoollenmills.com.au

by Briony Hand Dyed yarn
www.bybriony.com.au

Cascade Ultra Pima Cotton
www.cascadeyarns.com

Durable Yarn
www.durableyarn.com

Erica Knight Yarn
www.erikaknight.co.uk

King Cole Yarn
www.extraordinaryyarns.com
www.kingcole.com

Great Ocean Road Woollen Mill Yarns
www.gorwm.com.au

Katia Yarns
www.katia.com

Paintbox Yarns Cotton DK
www.paintboxyarns.com

Patons Yarn
www.ausyarnco.com.au

Rico Design Yarn
www.rico-design.de/en/home/

Scheepjes Yarns
www.scheepjes.com/en/

Stylecraft Yarn
www.stylecraft-yarns.co.uk

Tarndie Yarn
www.tarndie.com

Vinni's Colours
www.vinniscolours.co.za

White Gum Wool
www.whitegumwool.com.au

Wool and the Gang Billie Jean Yarn
www.woolandthegang.com

Yarn and Colours Must Have Cotton
www.yarnandcolors.com

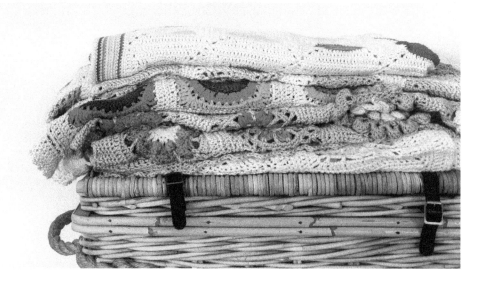

Alternative Yarn Colour Contributors

Alia Bland
www.thelittlebee.co.nz

Dedri Uys
www.lookatwhatimade.net

Emily Littlefair
www.theloopystitch.com

Jane Balke
www.yarnbombersunited.weebly.com

Julie Harrison
www.littlewoolliemakes.com.au

Mandy O'Sullivan
www.redagapeblog.com

Marianne Dekkers-Roos
www.marrose-ccc.com

Michelle Robinson
www.poppyandbliss.com

Pony McTate
www.instagram.com/ponymctate

Rachele Carmona
www.cypresstextiles.net

Robyn Hicks
www.yummyyarnandco.com.au

Sandra Eng
www.mobiusgirldesign.com

Sarah Shrimpton
www.annabooshouse.blogspot.com.au

Susan Regalia
www.instagram.com/suregal27

Useful Links

Yarn standards
Help to compare yarn weights
www.craftyarncouncil.com/weight.html

Hook standards
Hook size conversion chart
www.craftyarncouncil.com/hooks.html

Yarn Equivalents
Want to find an alternative yarn? This site compares
and gives you many possible matches
www.yarnsub.com

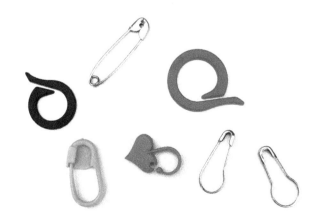

Acknowledgements

This book could not have happened without the love and support of my family - my hubby Stu and my girls, Megan, Erin and Brenna. You put up with my head in my computer and yarny mess as I wrote and made what I needed to. Thank you for looking after yourselves (and me!) while I was so busy.

Thanks to the amazing team who helped make my book come to life. You may not have met or even know each other, but to me, you're all part of my A Team. Thanks, Michelle Lorimer, for your sensational graphic design work. Thank you, Jo O'Keefe, for the simply stunning photography. Thank you, SiewBee Pond, my technical editor and proofreader extraordinaire, who took care of all the minute details, checking every word, character and space many times over, as well as making sure all the patterns were the best they possibly could be. Thanks to Amy Gunderson, the amazing hero who created all the charts. You really are a wonder woman, Amy!

My pattern testers played a huge role in the creation of this book. They tirelessly tested and re-tested the patterns, charts and projects. So much work for which I am forever grateful. Thank you, Barbara, Bek, Betty, Bonita, Chantelle, Isabel, Judy, Kalpana, Laurene, Lea, Lyn, Meghan, Monica, Nicole, Petrina, Rita, Samantha, Sharon, Shona, Stephanie, Tammy RP, Tammy T, Tharana and Vanessa.

Thank you to my crochet friends from around the world who made squares in their colours for me to include. Your colour choices are all fabulous and very you. My book is so much richer for your involvement. You're all stellar examples of the wonderful world-wide crochet community. Thank you, Alia, Dedri, Emily, Jane, Julie, Mandy, Marianne, Michelle, Pony, Rachele, Robyn, Sandra, Sarah and Susan.

A huge thank you to Judy, Sam and SiewBee for helping me by making some of the projects. Judy made the Melbourne Shawl, Sam made the Cirque Baby Blanket and helped with the Blossoming Flowers Blanket, and SiewBee made the Dahlia Scarf. You'd still be waiting for this book to happen without the expert swinging of their hooks! Thank you, Sally Coffey, for being my beautiful model, and adorable baby Campbell Simpson for modelling the Cirque Blanket.

Thank you to Bendigo Woollen Mills for supplying so much yarn for me to play with and create with. All of the cream samples, many of the alternative colours and projects are made with their delicious cotton. Thank you to the Great Ocean Road Woollen Mill for supplying the yarn to make the Killarney Blanket (p99). Thank you, Extraordinary Yarns, for supplying the yarn for the Blossoming Flowers Blanket. Thanks to Paintbox Yarns for supplying the yarn for the Prism blanket, Scheepjes for supplying the yarn for the Dahlia Scarf and the Melbourne Shawl; and Yarn and Colours for supplying the yarn for the Radius Coasters. Thank you, Briony, for dyeing the yarn for the Sunshine Cowl just for me.

And finally, a huge thank you to all the folks from all around the world who've made one or more of my patterns, my students, my newsletter readers, the wonderful folks who follow me on social media. You all so enthusiastically embrace my crochet designing. All of you encourage and support me with your endless kindness and eagerness. You keep my hook moving!

xx Shelley

About the Author

Shelley Husband is an Australian crochet designer and crochet teacher living on the south west coast of Victoria with her hubby and teenager in a tiny dot of a town by the ocean. Her two older children have left the nest and are spreading their own crafty and arty wings out in the world.

Shelley has crafted most of her life, trying "all of the crafts" over the years. These days, she spends most of her time with a crochet hook in hand. Having discovered a natural knack for crochet about six years ago after a break of a few decades, she hasn't looked back, creating hundreds of Granny Square patterns.

Shelley loves nothing more than designing new patterns aiming to extend her own and our crochet skills, gently challenging and encouraging us to create timeless, classic pieces sure to be admired and appreciated.

Seamless crochet is a real passion and she has many tips and tricks to make our crochet look the best it possibly can, using techniques she has combined and tweaked over the years.

When not designing crochet, you can find Shelley teaching crochet in workshops around Victoria and beyond. For those who can't make a workshop in person, she teaches worldwide via her annual Crochet-A-Long projects through her blog and YouTube channel. There's no doubting Shelley's passion for all things crochet.

You can find Shelley online at www.spincushions.com and on most social media channels as spincushions.

Find Shelley's other print books, Siren's Atlas and Beneath the Surface at your favourite online book retailer.

Find Shelley's ebooks on Amazon, iTunes and Kobo
- Granny Square Crochet for Beginners
- More than a Granny
- More than a Granny 2
- Flowers Abound
- Fran Crochet Blanket
- Greg Crochet Blanket
- Kaboom Crochet Blanket
- Mayan Crochet Blanket
- Siren's Atlas
- Beneath the Surface

9 780648 349709